# HOPE IN ACTION

## A Memoir About the Courage to Lead

## SANNA MARIN

SCRIBNER

New York Amsterdam/Antwerp London
Toronto Sydney/Melbourne New Delhi

Scribner
An Imprint of Simon & Schuster, LLC
1230 Avenue of the Americas
New York, NY 10020

First Scribner hardcover edition November 2025

SCRIBNER and design are trademarks of Simon & Schuster, LLC

Simon & Schuster strongly believes in freedom of expression and stands against censorship in all its forms. For more information, visit BooksBelong.com.

For information about special discounts for bulk purchases, please contact Simon & Schuster Special Sales at 1-866-506-1949 or business@simonandschuster.com.

The Simon & Schuster Speakers Bureau can bring authors to your live event. For more information or to book an event, contact the Simon & Schuster Speakers Bureau at 1-866-248-3049 or visit our website at www.simonspeakers.com.

INTERIOR DESIGN BY KARLA SCHWEER

Manufactured in the United States of America

10 9 8 7 6 5 4 3 2 1

Library of Congress Cataloging-in-Publication Data has been applied for.

ISBN 978-1-6680-6963-9
ISBN 978-1-6680-6965-3 (ebook)

To my daughter Emma,
and all the girls who
will change the world

# NOT A TYPICAL POLITICIAN, AND NOT THE ONLY ONE

**In December 2019,** at the age of thirty-four, I became the prime minister of Finland. At the time, this made me the youngest serving head of government in the world, and the head of a coalition government made up of five parties, all led by women. Four of us were under the age of forty. What most people want to know next is how that happened.

While it wasn't an accident that I reached a high position in politics after working intensely within my party, the Social Democrats, for over a decade, I didn't expect such a quick rise in my career, or intend it. I expected and intended to have a more normal path in politics, if a career in politics can ever be considered normal. One way to tell this story is the personal narrative: where I grew up, what my parents taught me, my first protest, my first campaign, how I won the prime minister election, what it felt like to have the responsibility of an entire government on my shoulders. But I will admit that I often find it uncomfortable to speak, or write, much about my personal life and history. This is not because I find it painful, or embarrassing, but because I want to focus on the issues that are important to the collective. I don't think that I made it to the top of the political pyramid because I was exceptional, but because I represented issues and values that are widely shared.

I came to politics at a moment in history when the old ways of doing things were being upended, from the way we report and share news to the way we understand global challenges. People with more unconventional backgrounds were slowly being accepted into the political mainstream. But it also wasn't an obvious career choice for me; growing up I thought of politicians mostly as older men in gray suits debating technicalities—a world that was very distant from the one I came from.

At first, I didn't know if there was space for me in the political system. I am not the only person who has felt that way. Although the space may have ended up feeling cramped at times, I'm glad I fought for it, because it means that other people might be able to come along and expand it. I prefer to look at issues and events from the perspective of movements, history, ideology, and the collective; my role was to contribute my skills and experience to do my part to make progress, not to be a "female leader," as I was often called. I think the conditions that produce an individual "female leader"—and the work she does in the role—are more important than how she felt, and certainly more important than what she wore.

The story of how I became the prime minister and led a government of five female leaders is also the story of a country, Finland, which has lately been celebrated across the west for its advancements in equality, sustainability, and the welfare model as well as resilience— all things that made me want to become a politician in the first place. Although Finland can't always live up to the image of our country as a kind of wintry, egalitarian utopia where, according to surveys, the happiest people in the world live, I am proud of my country, and I'm glad I got the chance to serve it. I am proud of my country because it is home to a strong social welfare system that has fostered a deep trust and solidarity in our society. It's this trust that allows us to move forward. While conservative politicians may say that social democratic policies prevent freedom, they are actually what give us our freedoms: to live securely, to be educated, to work to earn a fair wage, to have time to enjoy your family and friends, to be who you are. When a country makes these rights available to all its citizens, it makes it possible for every child to become anything they want and for people to live their fullest lives.

But these structures need constant upkeep and reforming; we cannot take them for granted. Every generation has the responsibility of recognizing and updating what came before them. We owe it to those who fought for our rights in the past and to the new generation who will need our support in the future.

○

When I was elected prime minister, I had no idea what was in store for me. In addition to all the typical responsibilities of a European prime minister—legislative debates, budget negotiations, navigating standard political disputes and pitfalls, and coordinating with the European Union—the global crises that came to a head during my term were historic. Within just over three months of my taking office, the world shut down in response to the COVID-19 pandemic, which required the ability to make unprecedented decisions with very little knowledge at first, the means to lead resolutely in an extremely complex environment, flexibility, communication skills, and, maybe above all, endurance. The stakes were incredibly high, and we knew the repercussions of our decisions would reverberate for years.

Then, just two years later, Russia started a full scale invasion of Ukraine, delivering a blow to the whole European security architecture and international rules-based order. Finland's longstanding policy of staying militarily nonaligned had to be re-evaluated and revised— quickly. We share a long border with Russia, and we could not leave ourselves, and the EU, vulnerable to aggression. This meant that we, the state leadership, had to lead Finland through the membership accession process for the North Atlantic Treaty Organization, NATO, at an accelerated pace.

My term as a prime minister, as you may remember, was also colored by a few scandals, harmless to some and outrageous to others, like the infamous clip of me dancing. One of the things I learned firsthand is that our political systems struggle to acknowledge that politicians are also human. At worst this alienates people from participating and running for office as they might fear that they won't fit into the narrow stereotypes of being a politician. This is the reason why it has been important to me not to change who I am even in the middle of the harshest media scrutiny. We need people from all backgrounds to engage in politics to build a society that is inclusive and resilient.

I'm writing this book not to memorialize myself—my triumphs or setbacks—but to share the importance of values—to show that insisting on what is right, even when it's difficult, can be a source of power and a guiding force in this broken world. If my personal story is relevant, it's because it shows what can happen when you refuse to accept what is wrong. From the day I stepped forward as prime minister of Finland, I have refused to accept the traditional mold of a head of government—even when critics screamed in protest. When we start upholding traditions over values, we stagnate, even fall apart. But when we stand up for our values, we pave the way for change—for a world where you can, yes, dance freely when the day's work is done.

# 1.

# DO I REALLY HAVE TO DO THIS?

**Just one year before I became prime minister,** I was serving my first term in parliament. I was there representing my region, Pirkanmaa, where I grew up and attended university. I was already a nationally known politician, having gained the most votes in my region in the 2015 parliamentary elections. Since 2013, I had been serving as the chair of the city council of Tampere, Finland's third-largest city. In addition to these duties, I was also the first vice chair of my party, the Social Democrats, which meant I was helping the party prepare for the upcoming parliamentary elections that would take place in April 2019.

After years of stagnation, the Social Democrats had been updating our policies to better reflect our values and create a progressive program for the future of the country. As one of the party leaders, I had been deeply engaged in this work and campaigned across Finland getting the word out to voters. This was the right job for me; I loved it. The 2019 elections felt like the moment a lot of our hard work would pay off, or could. For the first time in twenty years, the Social Democrats had a good chance of winning the most votes of any of Finland's parliamentary parties (nine at the time). In a parliamentary system where no single party ever has a majority, this means that our candidate for prime minister would lead negotiations on the formation of the government, which would consist of several parties. I was very proud of what we had accomplished, and ready to campaign tirelessly all winter and spring.

Then, around Christmas 2018, something horrible happened: Antti Rinne, the party leader, fell severely ill while on a holiday in Spain. This wasn't the flu. He was rushed to intensive care and put in a medically induced coma for two weeks due to a heart condition. Rinne was our candidate to become the next prime minister, but no one knew when, or even if, he would recover. Shortly after we heard the news that he was in the hospital, I got a devastating phone call from the second vice chair of our party, Maarit Feldt-Ranta. Her previously beaten cancer had come back, and the prognosis wasn't good. She had to withdraw from work and the campaign immediately.

Two of my close colleagues were fighting for their lives, and the whole party was in shock. As the first vice chair—first in line after Rinne—it was my responsibility to take the lead for the campaign just a few months before the national elections. I was troubled, and not just by leading the campaign but by the possibility of what could happen afterward. If I managed to maintain the party's growing support for the next few months, we would win. I would have no choice but to lead the governmental negotiations as our prime minister candidate. While I knew our program like the back of my hand and had a good amount of experience with public speaking and television debates, I did not feel ready. But we couldn't let the party lose its momentum, so I had no choice but to step up.

There was no time to panic: the campaign had to continue, and voters needed to see that we had everything under control—that the internal crisis threatening the party wouldn't overwhelm us. That January, we hosted a big launch event for the election campaign. We intended it to be a celebration that rallied everyone—party officials, candidates, and campaign workers from across the country—around the effort we were about to undertake together.

Initially, the mood was dejected. As people arrived in the large conference room in a high-rise seaside hotel in Helsinki, they looked sad and confused. It was as if they had already lost all hope. Until then, our party had been leading in the polls, but now the media—and all other political parties, which were eager to pull ahead of us—were expecting our support to crater. This launch had to convince everyone we could still win. When I approached the podium to give my speech to hundreds of party members, I knew it was a crucial moment for us. The atmosphere was genuinely dismal, and we had to turn things around, fast. I had to look and sound like a leader who would bring us to victory.

My speech had to accomplish two things: first, to articulate the sadness, anxiety, and futility everyone in the party was feeling, and second, to transform those feelings into a will to fight. I needed to rebuild the party's confidence so we could convince the voters that we deserved their trust. I hadn't written down my speech; I wanted to speak from the heart. I knew what to say because I was going through the same feelings they were. I spoke about what had happened and outlined the situation without embellishment, and then I outlined our plan to overcome the hardships and prevail in the upcoming elections. We had a job to do for our country and our citizens: in the decade to come, we would rebuild Finland as a nation that would be economically strong, socially just, and environmentally sustainable. Despite the setbacks, we could achieve this if we worked together as a team.

I noticed that the atmosphere in the room changed. People had arrived at the event thinking things were hopeless, but they left feeling motivated, energized, and even excited. It may sound sentimental, but the truth is that belief is essential to success: you must believe you can do something before you can achieve it. After the event, people kept coming up to me to express their gratitude and encouragement. The response gave me strength to continue. I realized that building confidence in others gave me the self-confidence that I desperately needed.

There can be a strange comfort in a crisis. With no time for feeling or deliberation, you simply do what needs to be done. I had always considered myself first and foremost a foot soldier of the Social Democrats; I'd joined the party at age twenty-one, and while I was surprised when I was asked to run for the position of vice chair, I thought of myself as a representative of a bigger movement, and a megaphone for the party's platform. Now, for the first time, I understood what it meant, and what it takes, to lead. I campaigned; I participated in debates; I met voters across the country. And to my surprise, even though our candidate for prime minister was in the hospital and I woke up every day daunted by the possible future, the support for the party was strong. In fact, it grew. While I dreaded the thought of becoming prime minister, I knew what I had to do, and I did it to the best of my ability (even while I also hoped Antti Rinne would recover and return).

To my relief, he did. Rinne was released from the hospital and returned to work about a month before the elections. But he was still physically weak. He had a hard time walking, and he didn't sound himself in public appearances. Many people doubted he was fit to lead the country. Our support started to decline. Now we were holding our breath with every new poll. During this period, when I traveled the country to campaign for the party and for Rinne, voters told me repeatedly that I should have remained the leader. While I was proud of the job I'd done under dire circumstances, the situation was uncomfortable. I supported our leader and always respected the chain of command within the party. But the voters were telling me how they felt. Deep down, I was afraid we would lose the elections.

And we nearly did. In the middle of April 2019, Finnish citizens voted in a parliamentary election, and the SDP won the most seats—but by just 0.2 percentage points. If the elections had been a week later, we probably would have lost. Nevertheless, we became the largest party in Finland for the first time since 1999; there would be a Social Democrat prime minister for the first time since 2003.

Once we began the negotiations to form a new government, the mood shifted. If Rinne struggled in the spotlight, he showed his strength in these talks. It was easy to get the Greens, the Left Alliance, and the Swedish People's Party to negotiate with us—they are all liberal parties—but it wasn't enough to form a majority government. We also needed the Center Party to participate in these talks so that we could accomplish our progressive center-left agenda; having a right-wing party in our government would prevent us from pursuing our key reforms, which focused on welfare, education, sustainability, jobs, and growth. The Center Party—who had been in power, with the prime minister seat, during the previous term—lost hugely this time around. They weren't inclined to join ours or any government for that matter. It was a major achievement that Rinne was able to convince them to engage with and join us. With this coalition we would be able to negotiate our priorities into realities. We were ecstatic.

Antti Rinne's government was appointed in June of 2019, a month and a half after the elections, we began our work. To my surprise, I was named the minister of transport and communications. I wasn't surprised that Rinne offered me a seat in the government—I had gained the most votes among the Social Democrats, and had successfully led our campaign during his illness, I had also been loyal to him for years, a quality that is very important in politics. But I had little experience with transport and communication; I had hoped to be appointed minister of climate and the environment, which were issues I'd been working on for years. Nevertheless, I of course accepted his offer, and became more enthusiastic about the role as I learned more about its mandate and responsibilities. It was a challenging position, with a sufficient budget, and there was a lot of overlap with climate issues. And above all, every day I went to work relieved I wasn't the prime minister.

○

I know why I felt unsure of leading a national government at that moment in my life. But in retrospect, I wish I hadn't been so afraid of the prospect. Women often feel they cannot take on a responsibility—whether it is a project or a new promotion at work, or an entirely new role—without being completely, perfectly prepared. We often have an image in our minds of the ideal way we would approach a situation, and when reality doesn't line up with that image, we hesitate. There are advantages to this approach. We are often more organized, and make fewer mistakes, when we have enough time to let reality catch up to our expectations. But the perfect moment to take action rarely, if ever, arrives, and in the meantime, the fear of failure or of not living up to expectations doesn't help. I've found that the best advice is that if you put your heart and mind into something, you will almost certainly adapt and grow to the task.

I was grateful to have learned this lesson early, because I would need it again soon. The SDP's celebratory moment was short-lived. Rinne had a difficult first few months in office. Our support dropped from 17.7 percent to 13.2 within six months, and things only got worse for him that autumn.

There were a few collective bargaining negotiations taking place in Finland during Rinne's term. Among them was the debate within the state-owned company Posti Group Oyj, which handles postal and logistic services in Finland. The main issue was that the company's leadership had decided to transfer seven hundred employees to an affiliate company earlier in the year. This meant these workers would receive lower salaries and worse working conditions. Strikes followed that fall.

Politically, this burdened the government and especially our party, as we have always represented the working class. On top of that, Rinne had previously served as a trade union leader, so he was particularly invested in the matter. Thinking he could help resolve the tensions between the workers and the company, he instructed the minister for ownership steering, Sirpa Paatero, to intervene in the company's policies, contrary to good governance principles. This was of course unacceptable. According to these principles the owner can change the company board and leadership, but it can't intervene in direct management and concrete decision-making within the company: this is the task for the board and the CEO.

Rinne's involvement caused a scandal. On one hand, he felt pressure to intervene in the collective bargaining negotiations and protect workers' rights; on the other, the state was obligated to follow the established protocols. Already on his back foot because of our lagging support numbers, Rinne became a perfect target. The Center Party began to criticize him harshly, and the newspapers smelled blood. Chaos ensued. People with a variety of political motives tried to take advantage of the instability. And then Rinne made some more unfortunate mistakes, as many people do when they're pressured from multiple sides and feel like they're losing control. He trusted the wrong people within our own party, who advised him based on their interest in replacing him. I tried to warn him, but I don't think he understood the gravity of the situation until it was too late.

It felt like witnessing a car crash in slow motion. I had tried to focus on my own work and not to get too involved. Hoping everything would cool down, I supported Rinne as a prime minister and as our party's leader. But then, at a question hour in parliament held in late November, it hit me: this was going to end badly. Rinne and Paatero were being questioned on the scandal, and something about their answers sounded off. I don't remember exactly what was said, but alarm bells began to ring in my head. As soon as the session was over, I went back to the Ministry for Transport and Communication and called my closest advisors to my office. The situation was serious, I told them, and even if our aim was to do everything in our power to make sure Rinne and the government survived the scandal, we needed to be prepared for what might happen if they didn't.

The next day, Paatero resigned, saying she couldn't do her job if she had lost the trust of the prime minister. This messaging only made things worse for Rinne, and her resignation wasn't enough to quash the criticism. The Center Party issued a statement saying they didn't trust Rinne to continue serving as prime minister, and they demanded his resignation. This wasn't just an empty threat: if the Center Party was serious, they could pull out of the government, which would mean we would lose our majority in parliament. The government would collapse.

○

From then on, things happened fast, and the atmosphere in the government was chaotic. All the other coalition leaders supported Rinne as prime minister. But the Center Party wanted to replace him. Their insistence on this was the result of several factors. Rinne's behavior during the postal scandal was the most obvious one, but there was much more to the story. Because the Center Party had lost so much support in the elections that spring, there had been debate and controversy over whether they should participate in Rinne's government. Many of their key figures were firmly against it and thought that the party should regain its support in the opposition. They also felt ideologically insecure in the center-left government after leading a center-right government, as they represented different views on several issues, especially from the Greens and the Left Alliance. Their status in the coalition remained a sore point in the party for the four-year term that would follow, causing disruptions and tensions that affected the entire government.

It may sound petty, but I think there were also historical reasons why the Center Party was so keen on replacing Rinne. In 2003, the Center Party won the parliamentary elections in a very tight race with the Social Democrats—by 0.2 percentage points, the same margin we won by in 2019. Before this 2003 election, we'd been in power holding the prime minister seat for eight years; after this election, the Center Party, the Social Democrats, and the Swedish People's Party formed a coalition government. Because they won, their leader, Anneli Jäätteenmäki, was appointed as the first female prime minister in Finland's history. But her term didn't last long. After two months, she had to resign because of a scandal involving leaked confidential documents about Finland's position and involvement in the war in Iraq; she was criticized for using these documents, and then later lying about it, to accuse the Social Democratic prime minister Paavo Lipponen of exceeding his mandate, leading to his defeat. The Social Democrats were furious, and they demanded she resign. The Center Party had to choose a new prime minister for the government. So now, after sixteen years, it was payback time. Rinne had to go.

As soon as I realized Rinne was in real trouble, my advisors and I started weighing what it would mean for our party and the continuum of the government, which we had heavily invested in. For me, it meant being ready to take the lead again if necessary. There was one other person in the party who might want the prime minister seat. Just a few years older than I am, Antti Lindtman was the leader of the parliamentary group—the official organization of SDP members in parliament—and very ambitious; we had known each other for years and worked together in the party leadership since 2014. We both had a wide base of supporters in the party, and it was evident that at some point we would run against each other, once it was time for the new generation to take the lead. The two of us are different in nature. If I had to characterize us, I would say that I am more ideological, whereas Lindtman is more tactical. If there were such a thing as a perfect politician, this person would have a combination of these traits.

As it became more and more certain that Rinne would step down, I started collecting supporters—people I knew would help me campaign, and whom I could count on for a vote. I was at an advantage because I was the first vice chair and first in line after Rinne. I had led our tense election campaign successfully, under significant pressure, and then gone on to win the most votes of any politician in our party, more than Lindtman or Rinne. I had served as the minister for transport and communications for the last six months. People trusted me.

Although I was still daunted by the prospect of becoming the prime minister, I was much more prepared than I'd been during the elections in April. For one thing, the idea wasn't completely new; I'd had to think about it a lot earlier in the year. Moreover, I had gotten experience at the highest level of government. I had traveled in my position and led negotiation tables. And perhaps most importantly, I had gained confidence in myself. I had faced very difficult situations and handled them with precision and determination. I was as ready as I would ever be.

Of course, government work did not stop while the scandal was unfurling. Nationally, the strikes in Finland had roiled the country; major foreign policy concerns demanded attention; and we were at the center of all discussions involving the European Union because Finland happened to hold the rotating presidency of the Council of the EU that fall. I was in Brussels leading a council meeting on transportation when I got a call from Antti Rinne that he would step down. As I was chairing the discussion, trying to finalize conclusions on some matter we were handling, the situation back in Finland was changing rapidly. The SDP was holding a meeting of party leadership immediately; I stepped outside the council meeting for a few minutes to participate. But I needed to get back to the meeting. I put in my AirPods to stay connected to the phone call in Finland and returned to chair the meeting. I asked my advisor and good friend Pirita Ruokonen to find me a plane back to Helsinki as soon as possible. We couldn't make it back until the next morning, so it meant a long night of waiting ahead.

When Pirita and I returned to the hotel in Brussels late that night, we knew this was it. I called my partner Markus Räikkönen, who was in Finland with our almost two-year-old daughter Emma, and asked him what he thought: Should I run? He answered very directly, with no hesitation: of course. It didn't surprise me. He had always been supportive of my career in politics and encouraged me to continue every time I doubted myself. Then I called my close supporters. They all agreed it was my obligation to run, and that they would support my decision to do so if I chose. It was now or never. I had to make the decision. We couldn't leave the government without a leader.

It was not a secret that I was a likely candidate to step in to lead the government—the press would be waiting at the airport when I returned to Helsinki. When we landed, I stopped at the ladies' room with Pirita, fixed my hair and makeup, and prepared to face the media. Emerging from international arrivals, I was ready. "I do not shy away from responsibility," I said to the crowd of reporters waiting with their cameras. "I am available for this position if the party decides."

The Social Democratic parliamentary group was having their weekly meeting at the same time. They were discussing the situation when Antti Lindtman, the leader of the group, must have been told I'd announced my candidacy right then. He stood up in the middle of the meeting he was chairing and left to address the media so as not to lose any time. He told them he was also available for the job. The campaign had begun.

According to procedure, in this type of situation, our prime minister candidate must be decided at a party council meeting, which has to be officially called. Sixty-one council members attend this meeting, and they would be the ones to choose between us. The meeting was scheduled for the following Sunday, the 8th of December, which meant we had just under a week to campaign from the day we learned Rinne would resign. In some ways, the party had been waiting for this election for years, because Lindtman and I represented such different paths. We each came with our own strong supporters, and we were also both well liked in general. Nobody had known the race between us would happen so suddenly, but we knew it would be tight.

As the clock ticked down, my supporters and I were constantly on the phone, attempting to get the majority of the sixty-one party members who would attend the party council to commit to vote for me. By the end of the week, our Excel spreadsheet was optimistic, though we also knew some people would have committed to voting for both sides. We were fairly certain we had been promised enough votes to win, but it would still be close. This meant that the final campaign speech I would give, which would take place just before the vote, would have to be convincing. It could decide the election.

Newspapers were all over the short campaign. Citizens were polled; council members were, too, though many didn't want to publicly commit to a side. I fared well in interviews, but I knew winning wasn't about overall popularity, but cold mathematics. Because the week of campaigning had been relentless, I didn't have time to write my speech until the morning of the meeting. But despite the stress all around me, I was calm and confident. I had no more time to worry about whether I was capable; I just had to do the best I could. I carried my small kitchen table to the middle of my living room to have more space around me and began to write.

This speech was the culmination of months of crisis and difficulty in the party, and because I had been at the center of the turmoil, I felt I could really speak to the emotional state of our members, and to the people of Finland more broadly. I wrote about the work we had already done and the responsibility we had to the citizens who had trusted us with their vote. I ended the speech with the words, "I trust you. Now is the time to be brave." I had a good feeling about it.

○

The auditorium in the parliament building was packed with members of the party and journalists who had been following the election. We only had one thing to decide: who would be the next prime minister of Finland. There was electricity in the air and everyone was nervous, except me. I knew that I would win. We had been working day and night, and I was sure that we had the votes. But it was something else, too; I have won and lost my fair share of elections, and this time I had a good feeling.

Here's how the process works: Everyone in the party remains in the same room. Each party member writes their vote on a piece of paper. Once all the votes are collected and counted, there is an announcement. Within an hour, we knew the result. It was closer than we had anticipated, but I had won by three votes.

At the last minute, Antti Lindtman told me his wife would be in the room for the vote. Markus and I did not live in Helsinki at the time. I'd bought a small one-bedroom apartment near the parliament building where I stayed when I was working, but otherwise I commuted to Helsinki from Tampere, a city about a two-hour drive north, where our family lived. Everything happened so quickly that I hadn't considered asking Markus to come to the vote. Though we had been together for many years, Finnish politics is less personal than politics in the US. It isn't as typical for spouses or partners to attend political events like this, even those of this scale. But of course now he had to come. Markus rushed to Helsinki so he could be with me for what would be one of the most surreal moments of my life.

He felt a bit awkward about all the attention, but I'm very glad he was there. It turned out to be important to have someone steady by my side. As soon as the vote was announced, I hugged Antti Lindtman and took the podium to give another speech, though this one was a bit less polished than the one I had delivered earlier that day. I spoke briefly to the press, and the photo illustrating the story of the election in the *New York Times* shows the emotions I was feeling: the look on my face is not exactly projecting easy confidence. Although I was confident of the outcome, I was also somehow in complete disbelief, awkwardly holding a bouquet and looking out of the frame. Behind me, the communication manager for the party had a look of shock on her face, too.

From there, the work began. We jumped right into preparing for the next four years. I went to a small meeting room near the auditorium because I had to select government ministers. The first person that I asked to take a seat in the government was my opponent Lindtman. He declined, wanting to continue as a leader of the parliamentary group after the tight race, which I understood. Sirpa Paatero couldn't continue as a minister for ownership steering after the postal scandal, but I offered her another post, which she gladly accepted. I also had to choose someone to take over my own position as a minister for transport and communication. This process felt a bit like playing Tetris, trying to fit each minister into their proper place as quickly as possible. By the end of it, everyone returned to the auditorium, where I announced the rotated responsibilities of our ministers and one new appointment—five women and two men.

Finally, at 9 p.m. the day was over, and a small group came back to my apartment. Once again, I was glad Markus was there, and my close and loyal colleagues in parliament, Suna Kymäläinen, Ilmari Nurminen, and Krista Kiuru, who also served as minister of family affairs and social services, joined us. The idea was that we might raise a toast before the work began again the next day. But as we gathered with our glasses of champagne in my living room, the feeling of shock returned. So many people were behind me, supporting me. I really couldn't let them down. I was suddenly the representative of an entire movement, both in the party and in Finland: I had just been granted power to shape the future of the country.

I didn't know what was coming. All I could think was: *Do I really have to do this now?* Of course, we all knew the answer. Yes.

# 2.

# COLLECTIVE BEGINNINGS

**When I woke up the next morning,** the media attention had already begun. Finland is a small country; our elections usually don't merit
more than a short news item in the international press. We hadn't
expected that within twelve hours of the vote, my communications and media advisor's phone would be ringing so much that
she couldn't use it. The scale of interest was unbelievable. I regret-
ted that I hadn't thought to delete the few baby photos of Emma
that I had posted on my Instagram account. The pictures themselves
didn't show much, but still I would have preferred they not appear
in the international press. (Ever since, I have been extremely cau-

tious not to put her in any situation where her privacy would be compromised.)

In retrospect, the conditions for a media firestorm around the election of a thirty-four-year-old, left-liberal, female prime minister are easier to see. In late 2017, the #MeToo movement spread from the United States abroad, and women's rights in the workplace became a major issue. What had started as a movement to stop sexual harassment in the American entertainment industry transformed into a worldwide reckoning in many areas, including politics. What many feminists had been saying for years was becoming accepted as common sense: the relative lack of female politicians was harmful to women's rights broadly. Meanwhile, the rise of far-right populism in the West, and particularly the election of Donald Trump as president of the United States, was worrying to people across the political spectrum. Jacinda Ardern had been elected prime minister of New Zealand about two years before I took office, and the media was similarly enthusiastic—or just fascinated by—the fact that a liberal woman in her thirties might lead a national government. Like me, she represented an image of a political leader that people weren't familiar with. In Finland, when I took office, the sense that women were finally getting our due was even more stark: five of the major parties in our new government were led by women, and four of us were under the age of thirty-five.

For much of the West, who knew little about our country, Finland suddenly became a symbol of progress, and even a light in the dark. But the reasons Finland was able to occupy this role abroad are complex. Articles reporting how happy Finns are, on average, regularly circulate in international media, and the Nordic welfare model that we follow is often cited by left-wing economists and theorists as the gold standard of social democracy. Although we have our problems, I am not here to try to disprove our reputation as a society that can boast relative happiness, social justice, and equality. I am proud of my country and am genuinely grateful that I have been able to serve it. This is not just theoretical for me; it is personal. The structure of Finnish society, and especially the Nordic welfare model, is the reason I was able to attend university, get involved in local politics, and eventually become a politician. Even though I hadn't considered a career in politics until I was in my twenties, many of my early experiences showed me how humane policy can change the course of a person's life.

○

I was born in Helsinki, but my family moved to Pirkkala when I was seven years old—the same age that my daughter is as of this writing. Pirkkala is a small town near Tampere, the city where I later started my political career. Pirkkala was a good place to grow up and go to school, and I lived there until I was nineteen. It is a middle- and upper-middle-class town where people play a lot of outdoor sports; nature is reachable in all directions. In the town center, there is a very old farmhouse, a horse stable, and an animal pasture. I consider myself lucky to have spent my childhood in a town like that, but at the same time it was obvious that my family wasn't typical there.

I was raised by my mother and her female companion in a small and very modest two-bedroom rental row-house apartment. Most of my friends lived in big houses with big yards, and everyone could see that we came from different social classes. But it didn't matter, because even if I didn't have the same background of wealth, I still had the same opportunities to become educated and pursue my dreams.

I could spend the rest of this book going through the difficulties that the women in my family have endured, so I'll tell the short version here. My mother had a very humble upbringing. She was raised in an orphanage until the age of eleven, and at fifteen began working different low-paid jobs. At twenty, she met my father, and she had me within a few years. Their relationship was difficult and didn't last long; my father was an alcoholic, and when I was around two years old my mother left him to secure a better life for me.

When I talk about my father, or the absence of a father figure in my life, people often respond with compassion. They want to project a tragedy onto me. Growing up surrounded by families that are labeled as typical gave me a sense of being an outsider, but I don't remember feeling like I was missing something crucial. Over the course of my childhood my mother tried, many times, to arrange meetings between my father and me so that we could spend time together, but he wouldn't show up. He was struggling with his own problems. I can still remember waiting for him on a railway station platform and noticing my mother's sadness and anger on my behalf when he never came. He finally reached out when I was an adult, but after a childhood with not even a postcard on birthdays or Christmas, I was not inclined to build a relationship with him.

Meanwhile, my mother didn't have an easy life; she didn't have even a secondary-level education, and she worked all sorts of jobs to support us. When she was growing up, Finland didn't have the high-quality education system and programs that I was able to take advantage of. But even though she did not have access to higher-level education, and we didn't have a lot of money, she was interested in the world and society, and always supported my ambitions and curiosity.

In retrospect, I can see how Finnish economic history maps onto my experience of class. I was born in the mid-1980s, when the Finnish welfare state was undergoing a sort of golden era, being bolstered and developed. Social services provided very concrete assistance to families that needed it, like housekeeping and nursing help, and the daycare and schooling systems were well resourced. But the dissolution of the Soviet Union, and the bursting of the fiscal bubble in the 1990s, hit Finland particularly hard. Our export with Russia dropped 65 percent, and the financial deregulation and overheating of the economy in the 1980s led to a severe economic depression in the 1990s. Unemployment skyrocketed almost to 17 percent, the government cut basic services, a lot of businesses were bankrupted, and many people's lives were turned upside down.

Nevertheless, this was still Finland. While this period shows that we should never take the welfare state for granted—that it must be strengthened and protected with hard political work—it's true that we have a very stable economic model based on principles of equality: income redistribution, robust social benefits, gender equality, and participation in the labor force. And even if governments did cut services and imposed unfair and harmful policies during that period, we still financed research and development that enabled new innovations in the late 1990s and paved the way for growth, especially in the telecommunications sector and engineering. What I remember from this economic crisis, at an age when I couldn't understand much of it, was having to share our school workbooks and other supplies.

Everyone who was a child at that time can remember how we had to cut erasers in half and write our homework into our own notebooks instead of workbooks to save public money. It could have been much worse if Finland hadn't had a strong foundation of collective responsibility and belief in the public good.

Because I was lucky enough to be born in Finland, I was privileged. I was entitled to have similar opportunities in education than my wealthier peers. I had close friends and affordable hobbies—I loved the arts, dancing, and walking in nature. Although my mother had no education herself, she was very encouraging of my education—she always spoke to me about university as if it were a given that I would someday attend, and encouraged me to think about all the exciting things I would get to do when I grew up. She always said to me that I could do and be anything if I put my mind into it.

I didn't get to travel much because we didn't have that kind of money, but I was interested in different countries and cultures. I remember my mother bought me books on special occasions about ancient civilizations, and I devoured any information I could find about art history. I also remember loving *Globe Trekker*, the long-running British travel TV show featuring young hosts who would visit destinations around the world and tell viewers about the local history and culture. And no matter your class background, growing up in Finland (and I think the same is true for other small countries) instills the idea of a wider world that is much bigger than your personal experience. It was inspiring to see the hosts of *Globe Trekker* traveling to places like Morocco or India and imagine that one day I might do the same. And despite how difficult I now understand my mother's life must have been back then, she was nothing less than attentive, loving, and encouraging. Above all, she showed me how to live openly: after she and my father split up, she eventually fell in love with a woman. This seemed completely natural to me at the time, and as a result I grew up with her and her female companion as my family, surrounded by friends from their queer community.

I know that my background is relatively unusual for a politician. Children who grow up working class or poor can't always see the opportunities that lead to success later in life, and they are often told, directly or indirectly, that they cannot achieve what their wealthier peers do. I'm not sure it occurs to many people from backgrounds like mine that they could grow up to become politicians. Of course, it would have been better and easier to have more money, but I learned very early on that some people are born with more resources and others with less, and that things are not fair by nature. We need to work together to achieve equality in our societies.

○

I went to a wonderful public elementary school. One of the things that made this school so great was that it was located next to a large, old forest. Finland doesn't have many natural resources, but we have a lot of forests that are a foundation of both our industry and exports, and the setting of the Finnish soul. In general, climate and biodiversity are very important issues to our citizens; we have an intimate relationship with nature, and it's not a coincidence that we are leaders in climate policy worldwide.

Because the forest was just next door, we often took field trips as a class to do things like orienteering and cross-country skiing, or just to explore. Outside school, I spent as much time in the forest as I possibly could, walking and playing with our dog, Coco. Some of my best early memories took place in this forest. It was an idyllic setting for a childhood, and it taught me the importance of preserving the environment before I even really understood it was in danger.

That changed when I was around eight or nine, and it was announced that part of the forest just next to our school was going to be cut down. The land was privately owned, and the owner had decided to sell the timber.

It was completely shocking for a young girl, and I was devastated. I didn't know what to do, but I wanted to do something. I really loved that forest, and it was inconceivable to me that it might disappear—that people might even consider cutting these trees down.

I wasn't alone in feeling this way—the destruction of this forest was a big topic of debate in our small town, and the school opposed the decision as well. But the debates didn't seem to have any effect, and this also distressed me. It was the first time in my life I remember experiencing the strong feeling of responsibility that has driven me throughout much of my career. I simply had to do something. Of course, I was just a kid, so my ideas for taking action were not especially sophisticated. Nevertheless, one day a few of my friends and I gathered on the road next to the forest, held up a Finnish flag, and began to sing the national anthem. It's possible we had the idea to block off the street—not that there was anyone there to see it. But we felt we had to do something, and that was the something we did.

There isn't a cinematic ending to this story: of course, we couldn't save the forest. The owner had the right to decide what to do with it, and they eventually razed the area.

If this was my first political experience, it was also the first time I experienced a kind of political defeat. And although it remains upsetting that one person could unilaterally decide to rob a community of a beloved shared natural space, this episode taught me not to get too discouraged. Rather than wallow in defeat, shortly after the forest was cut down, the school organized a campaign to help students plant new trees. This, too, was a formative lesson. I learned both how to accept a loss and how to move forward even after a setback.

○

I was the first person in my family to graduate from high school. At the time, this didn't feel remarkable, but I now see how, if things had gone a little bit differently, I might not have had so many opportunities. Like climate policy, education policy does feel personal to me, and I'm grateful to be able to use my perspective to advocate for the kinds of changes in education that might allow students like me, and those with fewer advantages, to flourish.

I eventually helped enact two changes in education policy that I was especially proud of. When the Social Democrats took office in 2019, education was one of the areas we targeted for reform. The previous center-right coalition government had cut funding to education as part of a broader policy of austerity—they had promised not to, but they ended up cutting education funding so much that it became a meme. As soon as our party formed a government in 2019, we set out to reverse those cuts, and more. Extending compulsory education from the age of sixteen to the age of eighteen had been in the Social Democratic Party program for many years. We had already tried to reform the secondary school system when we were in government and in charge of the ministry of education and culture during the years 2011–2015, but the reform faced resistance and we weren't able to deliver. While most students did finish high school, or attended a vocational school to finish their studies, some still did fall through the cracks because schooling wasn't mandatory after age sixteen.

These individuals would then, statistically, struggle for the rest of their lives. They struggle to participate in the workforce and often have to remain on social benefits. From an economic perspective, this costs the state a lot of money. More importantly, from a human perspective, I believe it's critically important that the state do everything it can to prevent fifteen-year-olds—who are still children—from disadvantaging themselves for life before they can even vote.

Economists knew that decreasing the number of high school dropouts would boost the economy and increase employment. But once we made this change for compulsory schooling, we had to adjust other policies alongside it. If we were requiring schooling up to the age of eighteen, we had to provide books and other equipment for these students as well. Until then, books for younger students were covered by the state, but once schooling was "optional," students had to provide their own. In university there's no tuition, so university students could apply for benefits or subsidies to pay for their books, and it's relatively easy to find university reading assignments in the library—it was only in secondary school that this created a problem.

Providing textbooks to high school students was admittedly not the biggest problem Finland faced in terms of combating inequality. But these small things can add up. For poor families, paying for schoolbooks could mean the difference between sending your child to high school or not. The more money your family had, the easier it was to purchase books. According to some reports, these books could cost up to two thousand euros during all of high school. Again, I remembered my own experience. As a high school student, I had to buy most of my books secondhand, and it was still very expensive; depending on the curriculum, some books you could only find new, at full price. I often had to borrow books from classmates, which was sometimes difficult because they needed the books as well. For students who attended vocational schools, the cost of supplies could add up—sometimes even more than textbooks.

There was more disagreement around this issue than there should have been. Opponents to the legislation argued that it would not be a wise decision economically and that teachers would have to follow a standard curriculum if they used government-funded textbooks, which some claimed would create a less efficient system in which high school teachers felt surveilled. I suspected, though of course no one would say this, that some opponents of the legislation also wanted to discourage students from poorer and more difficult backgrounds from attending high school, because they believed they were disruptive and caused problems in class.

Nevertheless, the Social Democrats were able to do as we promised, at least partially. I liked the wording of this part of the platform: We "restored the honor of education" by investing over one billion euros into the sector throughout our government term. It was an important step toward a more equal society, but also economically reasonable. Finland's economic success, competitiveness, and foreign trade is crucially linked to the level of competence and education of our people, and the biggest obstacles for economic growth are lack of a skilled workforce and productivity, which are fully linked to the performance of our education system.

Education reform wasn't the only big national item on our party's to-do list. Previous governments had tried and failed to accomplish major changes to our social and healthcare system that we were finally able to implement. While details may sound technical—we shifted control of social services and healthcare from municipalities to regions, allowing cities and towns of drastically different sizes to focus on education, vitality, land use planning, and other things they are in charge of—this was the biggest structural reform in Finland in decades, and our government was able to accomplish what several governments had tried to do for a long time. (And we did it in the middle of COVID—a topic I will return to later, though that time is still traumatic to think about.) Finland has an aging population and people are geographically unevenly distributed. Smaller municipalities had a lot of problems handling the social and healthcare services, especially tackling the constantly growing need for resources. Our administrative changes didn't solve the core problem that certain services will become strained as the population ages, but they spread out the burden.

○

A major reason we were able to accomplish everything we accomplished is because as a party, the Social Democrats never take the social safety net for granted, and we try to strengthen it at every opportunity. The social safety net in Finland has built the trust we have within our society. Our strong collective bargaining system allows people to trust that their employers won't take advantage of them; our welfare model means that if someone is out of work, they can rely on the state to cover their basic needs and keep them safe. Some in the center or on the right wing dislike the cost of these services, or they resent high tax rates on corporations and the wealthy. But a government does not operate in a vacuum; it must always be prepared for a crisis. And if we look at the depression of the 1990s or the pandemic just a few years ago, it's clear that a foundation of economic and social equality is necessary to allow both individuals and the collective to flourish. An equal, just society, in which everyone has the opportunity to live a good, honest life, is always going to be more resilient than an unequal one. If countries do not cultivate trust in their societies, and belief in institutions, then people are polarized; they feel as if they are disconnected both from each other and from the country as a whole. They do not feel they have any control over what happens in their society, and because they are themselves likely struggling, and so focused on their own problems, they lack the energy to participate in political activity. This is, of course, a way to keep power in the hands of the few and privileged.

Ultimately, I am grateful that what I took from my early experiences was a conviction that the circumstances of your birth should not determine the course of your life. From this perspective, of course, it's no wonder that I became interested in social democratic ideas and policies. As I grew up, I began to realize that I had always been passionate about certain issues; they were so enmeshed in my understanding of the world that I hadn't realized that many of my concerns were actually political in nature. Climate, human rights, and social justice were especially important to me. And as I looked around, at the news and what was going on in the world, I realized that I shouldn't take it for granted that someone would take care of these things for my generation. Change was slow, and crises were piling up. By the time I was in university, I felt deeply that it wasn't just my opportunity, but also my responsibility to help make change in society however I could. Do my own part, how small or big it might be.

# 3.

# JOINING THE MOVEMENT

**In high school, I knew I wanted** to go to university, but I didn't know what I wanted to study. I hadn't yet figured out what my passion was. In retrospect it seems inevitable that I'd go into politics, but I never considered it while I was growing up. When I heard the word "politician," I thought of men in gray suits looking distant and important—a totally different universe and reality from the one I lived in. I had never met anyone who had anything to do with politics; my family wasn't political, and none of my friends' parents were, either. They all had what seemed ordinary jobs, as teachers, engineers, small business owners, and so on. What happened in parliament, or even in local government, seemed far away. At one point, I remember I had the idea to study theology—I see now that this notion was based on an interest in how society is structured and how this affects people's lives, and not necessarily about religion itself. Still, it was short-lived; I started reading the entrance exam book for the theology program at the University of Helsinki just days before the test. Of course, I didn't get in. Still, I continued to study the subject after the exam, because of my interest in it (and because I had already bought the book).

After high school, I worked as an office clerk in the youth services section of the city of Tampere, where I had just moved with Markus. We met at the age of eighteen in a bar following my friend's house-warming party, and after a year of dating he came to me one day and announced he had rented an apartment for us in the city. I was a little surprised because we hadn't discussed moving in together, but I didn't take much convincing because we were very much in love and both ready to start lives independent from our families. Sitting in the office one day, I picked up a guidebook for the University of Tampere that featured all the majors and what they involved. Immediately, the idea of administrative science appealed to me. I was eager to learn more about how societies are constructed and maintained (or not maintained) and to understand the management and economics of organizations, as well as the legal foundations of administration. Because I had no idea what I wanted to do with my life, I also liked that the program seemed like it could apply to many different fields.

Although I was a little lost, I did have a strong feeling that I wanted to change the world. I just didn't know how to begin. In 2006, around the same time that I was thinking about my educational choices and planning to apply to the University of Tampere, I went to my first political meeting, for a Social Democratic youth organization in Tampere. Before this I'd read about several political parties' programs and policies, and I seriously weighed my options. I thought that this might be a way to meet people like me and learn a little bit more about how the political system worked on a local level.

But the meeting was a huge disappointment. I remember my first time walking into the local SDP headquarters, the Tampere Workers' Hall, a massive stone building in the center of the city. Feeling a little anxious, I climbed five flights of stairs to the party's youth organization office, and when I walked into the room everyone just stared at me. They couldn't believe that someone they didn't already know would want to participate. My family wasn't affiliated with the party, and at the time the party was stagnating, and didn't appeal to young people. It was unusual for a young person to develop interest in a political party independently, out of curiosity and general interest, without connections or being brought on by a friend or colleague.

Then, once the meeting started, to my surprise, the group wasn't talking about politics—they were debating whether they should pay for meals for the volunteers working at an event they were hosting. I couldn't believe it. This debate had no bearing on any of the major political issues our generation was facing. These were young people, my peers. Weren't we supposed to be the most passionate members of the political system? Where was the revolution? Instead, we were seriously discussing lunch (which they of course should have provided, without question or argument). I don't know if I should have laughed or cried, but I did feel more depressed than amused.

It took me a while to get back into local politics after that experience. Something about how unconcerned the organizers were about actual policy issues really bothered me. Though it left me feeling discouraged for a few months afterward, this moment eventually spurred my more concerted efforts to become politically active.

In 2007, I started university, where I did finally meet the people I was looking for. Several students in my major were involved in the student movement, party politics, and the Social Democratic Party, and I began spending time with them, going to their parties to talk about what kinds of projects and initiatives they were involved in. I also joined their reading groups. We read all the socialist classics—Marx, of course, but also figures like Eduard Bernstein, a reformist Marxist who was prominent in Germany's Social Democratic Party in the late 1800s and early 1900s; Karl Kautsky, a more orthodox Marxist (and Social Democrat) from the Austrian Empire; and writings by figures like the Austro-Hungarian anthropologist Karl Polanyi and an Italian philosopher and politician, Antonio Gramsci. It's never been my nature to take my political cues for the present from history books, but I wanted to do my homework, and these thinkers—especially Bernstein and Kautsky—come to mind now for the way they model different approaches to politics that are still visible in Finland today. Bernstein was more focused on establishing and spreading the political movement, not any specific cause or platform, while Kautsky was much more ideological and issue-oriented. I found both sides interesting, and I now know that both are important. I would later see this same dichotomy appear again and again in my own experiences with the Social Democrats, and although I tend to fall on the side of issues and ideology, I know that it takes both vision and strategy to effectively make change.

Today, my friends from university—and Markus—tease me about how much time I used to spend in the student café during breaks between class, debating anyone and everything. I've always been a very serious, focused person when it comes to politics, and I have a tendency to map out all the implications of any given argument and try to see the bigger picture. What will a certain energy policy mean for climate emissions and social justice? How will a specific economic reform affect unemployed people? I enjoyed debating and learning the narratives of different parties. My friends always joked that I was going to become a politician, but I could only really see myself as a public servant, someone who assisted or supported the party in its bigger goals. I didn't have the connections, money, or experience to understand how I might run an election, much less win. As a twenty-two-year-old, any kind of theoretical political future for me felt very far away.

I was also busy—I had been working since I was eighteen, and while at university, in addition to my studies, I always had a job on the side. While I was eligible for a student loan that would have allowed me to study without having to worry about paying for food and rent at the time, I couldn't trust that I'd be able to pay the loan back if something bad happened and prevented me from working later in life. I watched as students from wealthier backgrounds took out loans to support them during their studies, but it just didn't feel like an option for me. But I wasn't upset about it. That was just the way the world worked, and I was learning a lot as a salesperson in grocery and clothing stores, talking to customers. I have always considered all work valuable, as long as the conditions are fair.

○

In most cases, the first step to pursuing a career in politics is to join a political party. In Finland, we have eight to nine parties that make up the parliament. Because I had no background in politics, I had little sense of which one to join. But I knew I was leaning to the left and had liberal values, so I easily narrowed it down to three parties: the Social Democratic Party, the Green Party, and the Left Alliance. While I had spent more time with members of the SDP at university, I also shared a lot of the same values with the Greens and the Left Alliance. I cared deeply about the environment and was worried that the people in power weren't doing enough to combat climate change and biodiversity loss; on the economy, I believed in evening out the playing field for those of different means through equal education and good welfare services, and that fair taxation makes this possible for all. But the SDP has a much deeper understanding of how to build structures that allow these visions to become reality. What's more, the Social Democrats maintained strong connections abroad, and the ability to cooperate on the world stage was critical to all the issues I cared about most: climate, human rights, and equality. The party also played a key role in helping to build the Nordic welfare model, which was the primary reason that someone like me, from a more humble background, had the opportunity to go to university and consider getting involved in politics at all.

Unfortunately, my first Social Democrat Party meeting was a similar experience to the time I attended that youth organization meeting spent discussing who was buying lunch. It was boring, dusty, and out of touch—exactly as I'd imagined politics to be. For decades the Social Democrats had shaped our entire society, but now they were fixated on maintaining things as they were and not continuing to pursue change. Still, I liked the values the party represented, and it ultimately seemed like the right choice for me. The SDP is a much bigger, more powerful party than the other two left-liberal parties, which meant that, as a member, I might have the opportunity to actually make an impact on the issues I cared about. The SDP had shown their ability to take action; they weren't just talking about changes they wanted. It is easy to want change, but it is much more difficult to take concrete and effective action and accomplish it. Having spent some time with my classmates who were also in the party, I knew that there were opportunities for us to make some reforms, and I was excited about the prospect of actually shaping the party's future. Like many younger people at the time—this was the moment that Barack Obama had begun his campaign for president of the United States— I really wanted to take action, not just sit on the sidelines. Action felt both possible, and necessary.

○

So I joined the SDP. Very quickly, I went from having no idea what I wanted to do with my life to being completely obsessed with politics. I had never cared much about socializing and going out with friends, and now that I was in the SDP, I was spending all my time in party meetings and debating with my fellow students and people from different political parties. In the process, I learned a lot about the party's history, and I came to see exactly why we were in the situation we were in—and felt I could better understand how to help fix it.

The SDP has been a large party since Finland became independent from the Russian Empire in 1917, during the Russian Revolution. We are also the oldest active political party in Finland. Established in 1899 as the Workers' Party of Finland, we have always stood for the working classes, labor unions, and social rights like public schooling and healthcare. During Finland's golden age of welfare programs in the middle of the twentieth century, the SDP often worked together with the Center Party, a party that has historically represented farmers and people in agriculture, to develop progressive reforms. Between Finland's independence and the 1980s, the SDP had five prime ministers, most serving multiple terms, and we were almost always in the governing coalition.

Then came the 1990s: a tectonic shift in how people understood the world followed the fall of the Soviet Union and the global recession. In 1991, center-right parties won elections, and the SDP, previously a part of the governing coalition, became part of the opposition. Finland's economy plummeted through a combination of an overheated economy, a banking crisis, and the collapse of trade with the Soviet Union. The austerity policies that took over in Finland hit people very hard, and the heavy cuts to social services and benefits, along with the rising unemployment, were devastating.

As is common following crises, the people were dissatisfied with the government in power, which made everyday life hard for people trying to survive in the economic recession, and they wanted a change. After the worst of the depression abated, the Social Democrats won our biggest victory since World War II, and we stayed in power for eight years, from 1995 to 2003.

The SDP prime minister from this time, Paavo Lipponen, has a controversial legacy, both within the Social Democratic Party and beyond it. He had massive support, and he is still known as a strong politician and a respected statesman: although Finland applied to join the EU before he took office, he was the prime minister since our first months as a member state, and he firmly believed that we needed to be at the table when decisions that affect the whole of Europe were being made. He pursued expansionist and pro-integration policies and advocated for cohesion among the EU member states in a way that set Finland up for economic success in the rapidly globalizing economy. Finland became the only Nordic country to adopt the common currency and join the euro area when it was established in 1999. His government also invested in research and development, boosting the economy at the end of the 1990s, with help from the tech boom and the wild success of the Finnish telecom company Nokia. This was a departure from what the party had done for the previous decades—Lipponen was ambitious, and he had strong views about how Finland should participate in the changing world.

But on a national level, things were more complicated. While Lipponen was handling EU and international affairs efficiently, he also presided over heavy cuts to benefits and welfare, particularly during his first term, when the effects of the economic crisis still had to be managed. The right-wing parties that helped make up the coalition government in his first term led the country's discussions on how to balance the public finances to support the recovery of the economy. This meant cuts and more austerity. Finland was able to recover, but by his second term, Lipponen seemed to focus more on EU and international issues rather than reinvesting in welfare and policies based on our core values.

In 2003, after Lipponen's second term as a prime minister, the Social Democrats narrowly lost the election to the Center Party. We continued in government as the second-largest party, but after Lipponen stepped down as chair, we sank into the defensive stagnation that even I noticed as a twenty-two-year-old university student. We were so concerned with holding on to our slipping power that we offered voters little sense of the core values we represented. The Social Democrats became a somewhat out-of-touch organization, with few exciting ideas that might attract and inspire a younger generation.

By the time I joined in 2007, the party seemed intent on preserving decades-old achievements rather than proposing any new reforms, or taking risks. It seemed the party suffered from a lack of understanding about who we were and what we wanted to represent. While this was understandable, given how the welfare state was threatened during the 1990s and early 2000s, I knew we weren't on the forefront of innovation or particularly exciting to voters. We needed to build a movement based on support for the ideological growth younger people were craving. The Social Democrats cared about the environment and promoting and defending human rights. But our biggest strength has always been the welfare model that the Social Democrats had helped develop. This is what made my life path possible, as has been the case for so many people. I believed that we could dedicate time and effort to building something new on that foundation. I wasn't the only one. I was part of a growing consensus among various groups in and around the SDP: union activists, old-school socialists and reformers, and students and young intellectuals. We were all disappointed in the party, but for different reasons. And after years of dispiriting defeat, this group was poised to collaborate on something new.

○

In fall 2008, when I was twenty-two, I campaigned in an election for the first time. Although I had no experience, connections, or money, I really wanted to do something for my new home city, and for my new political party. I signed up for our party's election list for the city council and I ran my campaign just as you'd expect a university student running for local public office to run a campaign. Online campaigning and social media weren't widespread at the time, and I didn't have funding for advertisements or printing. Using Photoshop on my mom's laptop, I made my own very simple campaign flyers with a slogan "Four Targets for Four Years." I canvassed the city, approaching people in the street and at our party's campaign events.

I did not win a spot on the city council. But I did get 160 votes, about half of what I needed to be elected. This may not seem like a lot, but I was pleasantly surprised. I had just moved to the city, I was young, I didn't know anyone, and my campaign was incredibly modest. Still, 160 people voted for me. It was enough to motivate me to keep going, and it showed me that my values did resonate with some people—most of whom I'd never met.

I had already thrown myself into politics, but this election was the encouragement I needed—not only because some people had entrusted their vote to me, but also because people in my party had noticed how dedicated I was and appointed me to some positions in the city administration. I was nominated to be a deputy member of the city board, and a member of a group that was handling matters related to the city's personnel policy. These were good responsibilities for a newcomer that would teach me a lot about how a city government functioned, and I was surprised by the support I got from more experienced members in our party who encouraged and helped me. I went to every party meeting in my city and region that I could, I became very active in the youth organization and in the student movement, and I was an advocate for issues like human rights, equality, and climate and energy policy. I was reliable and hardworking, and more and more people started to notice this. Soon I found myself serving in national positions in the Social Democratic youth organization and in the party council in addition to my roles at the local level.

I was opinionated, and very vocal about my beliefs. Because of my mother and her friends in the LGBTQ community, I had strong views on same-sex marriage as well as trans rights. But my outspokenness was balanced with a strong dedication to the party. While I came to be seen as a critical voice and progressive in my stances, I was able to gain older party members' trust because I wasn't seen as just a critic, but as someone who cared about the party and was willing to do the work behind the words. Slowly but surely, I was given more opportunities.

Of course, I was not alone. In 2008, the global economic recession had galvanized a generation of young people, and even though the financial crisis had started in the United States, it hit Europe hard as well. Austerity politics had taken hold, and there was widespread concern about the direction the world was heading in, particularly among young people. In Finland, a dynamic and passionate cohort of young future politicians began to form, and I was part of it. For a long time there hadn't been such interest in youth politics, which were seen as training grounds for political parties. But gradually people in power were starting to wake up to the fact that young people were losing interest in party politics and traditional ways of engaging, and they needed to course correct.

Likely picking up on the generational shift happening around the world, the Finnish media began inviting youth organization leaders to participate in televised debates, which are common in Finnish politics, around 2010. By that time, I was a vice chair of the national Social Democratic youth organization, and when we received an invitation that the chair couldn't attend himself, he asked me if I'd like to go in his place.

I loved debating, so I enthusiastically agreed. My passion for issues was well suited to television—I was clear and straightforward, and I also wasn't afraid to *really* argue—and I loved the sense that I was speaking directly to people. I apparently did well, because the media began asking me to represent our party in these debates more and more.

Although it was unusual for young politicians to rise to national recognition, there were many prominent young politicians in different parties back then, and we were thrown together for these debates often. The National Coalition Party had several well-known figures in their organization, as did the Center Party and the Greens; Li Andersson, the youth leader of the Left Alliance, later became a close colleague of mine in our government. There was a sense that this generation would go far—we had new visions, and although we were in different parties, we undoubtedly challenged each other to grow.

○

In 2011, the SDP finished second in Finland's parliamentary elections and returned to government after four years in the opposition.

In addition to other key ministries, the first female leader of our party, Jutta Urpilainen, was appointed finance minister, which is the second most significant position in the government.

After years of hesitation and lackluster messaging, this was a turning point for our party. We were finally back in the government, and we needed to decide what path to take: Were we moderate, or were we strongly liberal?

For me, and many other young people in the party, this should never have been up for debate. Our values are freedom, equality, peace, and solidarity. But it was no longer a given that everyone in our party would truly fight for these values.

We were torn on many issues, and the party leadership didn't always understand what was important to our base—that people were craving progressive policies and a real vision for the future. Instead, we cut taxes on companies and took a hard-line stance against asylum seekers and migrants. Fears of losing our working-class support to the populist conservative right, the True Finns Party (now called the Finns Party), who had made surprising gains in these elections, made some people in the SDP skittish. This was visible also in our EU policy at the time of the euro crisis of 2011. While other member states acted out of necessity and solidarity, Finland became the only one to demand collateral from Greece to secure our contribution to the bailout package.

This fear, and the assumption that people were more conservative than they actually are, pushed our leadership to tread too lightly on value-based policy. From the outside, we didn't recognizably represent anything. Party leadership made tentative proposals on issues like same-sex marriage and trans rights, which I, like many others, was very vocal about. Young people had been losing faith in the party for years, and our stances on issues like these were a major reason why. Although clashes between the old guard and the new may have been better than the stagnation the SDP had been experiencing previously, we were undergoing an identity crisis.

○

In the meantime, another municipality election was coming up, and by now I had enough experience and backing to make a serious play for a seat on the city council. I still made my own flyers, but in every other way I was better equipped to win a campaign. In 2012, at the age of twenty-six, I was elected with slightly more than eight hundred votes—a significant increase since my first election.

But the real surprise was what followed. After the elections, I was nominated to be the *leader* of the city council, a position that I had never expected. It was very unusual for such a young person—I had just turned twenty-seven—to be given an opportunity to prove herself in that way. Until then, the chair of a city council was a prestigious position reserved mostly for senior members. It was a great honor to even be considered. And to everyone's surprise, I won the nomination out of three people from our party. I became the youngest person to hold that position in the history of Tampere.

Now, I don't want to diminish my accomplishments—I had proven myself a valuable member of the SDP and the community, and I was up to the task of being the city council chair. But there was more to my nomination, as there always is in politics. Beyond my dedication and skills, I had two other factors working in my favor. First, our party was hoping to attract more young people, and giving me this role ended up generating a lot of media coverage. Another not-so-flattering reason for my nomination was that the two other candidates had more opposition than I did, so I was a convenient compromise for some.

I really enjoyed the work, and it was around this time that I made politics more of a full-time job. Until then, I had spent every extra minute, and all my spare money, campaigning, working with the SDP youth organization, and participating in meetings and debates, but I had always maintained a job on the side when I was a university student. I was passionate about my duties on the city council: we managed to vote on several big investments that reshaped the city, making it a more attractive place to live and work for people around the country. Since then, Tampere is often named the number one city in Finland where people like to live.

I also fiercely defended the rights of the residents. For example, I opposed the increase in fees for leisure services, which would make life more difficult for low-income families, and gained a lot of support and attention over these issues. In the council chamber, I always tried to keep discussions moving in a direct, focused way, and I was composed but very determined. Because I was a young woman, I think people were surprised by how well I was able to control the conversation, and how strict I was able to be when needed. It helped that my studies had given me a solid foundation for the work, and I knew the legislation and guidelines concerning municipal administration quite well.

One Tampere city council meeting in particular became notorious around the country. In 2016, the major item on the agenda was the city's tram system, which we were planning to invest in alongside other major projects. Tampere is a large city by Finnish standards; it is the third largest city in the country, with around 260,000 residents. The city already had a fairly good public transportation system, but because its population was growing annually, we needed to invest even more in infrastructure, and building a new tram network was one of the ways to do this.

I was always strongly in favor of the project even though it was going to cost a lot. The long-term benefits outweighed the initial price tag, and having an efficient tram network would help the city reach its climate and welfare targets. But the investment also had strong opponents, falling mostly along party lines: the left-wing parties were in favor of the tram, and the center-right conservative parties were more divided, or against it. The Tampere tram was a hot topic both locally and nationally. Within the city council, the debate became so heated that two meetings became the subject of national news.

As the leader of the council, I had both admirers and detractors. But in this moment I was praised for my ability to take a firm hold of the conversation. I directed council members to stay on topic when they tried to expand their speech to other matters, but I also respected everyone's right to speak and stayed calm when many started to feel frustrated during the hours-long debate. My ability to perform in a high-stress situation caught the attention of many, especially in our party.

○

In 2014, two years before the tram discussion, Social Democrats held a party conference, also known as a congress, the regular meeting during which we elect our party leader, vice chairs, secretary general, and national bodies for party administration. Suddenly, I began getting phone calls from different people in the party all across the country encouraging me to run for the position of vice chair. It had been held by another young person before, and because the youth movement of the party had been gaining momentum over the last several years, many people in the party wanted someone who could continue to represent our views. Of course, I agreed that we should have more young people in these senior roles, but I was twenty-eight, and I hadn't even considered it, nor had I expressed interest in running.

Then, people in the Tampere chapter of the party started offering their support, saying they would vote for me if I ran. By this time, I felt a deep responsibility to the party, and it was the encouragement I needed. But the main reason why I decided to run was that I was dissatisfied with some of the policies that we had agreed on in the government. My main worry was that the austerity narrative we had adopted during the right wing–led coalition didn't offer a real choice for people in the upcoming parliamentary elections. Our support had dropped, and feedback from our voters was harsh. I had always represented a leftist view underlining countercyclical economic policy and the importance of investments to boost growth and employment, yet we participated in a coalition that was cutting services and education while giving tax breaks to corporations. Like many others in the party, I was frustrated with the direction that we were going, and there was a growing disappointment with the party leadership. As the party congress approached, we knew there would be challengers for several different positions. I would be among them.

Finally, at the party convention in Seinäjoki in 2014, the party

# 4.

# LEARNING CURVE

**The year after I was elected vice chair** of the Social Democrats, in 2015, Finland held its parliamentary elections. This was the second time I ran for a seat in parliament. In the previous election, in 2011, I didn't get nearly enough votes, but it was a learning experience. This time, though, I was serious. I had decided that I would not only win a seat, but that I would get the most votes within my constituency, Pirkanmaa. I had a good team, friends from university and people from our party, campaigning with me, and I'd built a reputation as a strong leader of the city council and as a person who defends what she believes in.

The SDP had been in government the previous term—from 2011 to 2015. But during the parliamentary elections of 2015, we performed badly, and we only received 16.5 percent of the vote. The center-right parties formed a government, and we became part of the opposition.

While the party's overall result was disappointing, I did win my district, by a significant margin with almost eleven thousand votes, and got the fourth most votes nationally of all the candidates running from our party. And even though I'd made a decision to aim high and put everything I had into the elections, I was surprised by the result. I was of course very happy about my own win—I'd spent almost all my time for eight years working for the party, and it was paying off. But at the same time the overall outcome of the elections was dispiriting.

After years of work, this was the moment for our party reckoning. If we were going to make a comeback in the next parliamentary elections, in 2019, we had to solve our identity crisis and reform the party platform for the future. Were we moderate or liberal? Protectors of the old structures or creators of new ones?

I wanted to be involved in outlining the new platform: this was what had excited me about joining the Social Democrats in the first place. In the meantime, though, parliament was like nothing I'd experienced before.

○

Parliamentarians work in groups associated with their political parties. Finland's electoral system is based on proportional representation: the number of members of parliament each party has is proportional to the total vote share that party received in a given region. I worked as a member of the Social Democratic parliamentary group, which held its meetings every Thursday, along with all the other groups in parliament.

I love our parliament building with its light gray granite facade and airy marble interior. It was designed by Finnish architect J. S. Sirén and it represents 1920s classicism, with art deco and modern elements; I think it is a very noble and beautiful building. I was so excited to be elected to parliament for the first time, and I wasn't alone. Even though the election results weren't what we'd hoped, several new members of the parliamentary group were under thirty years old, and we all had the sense that we were about to get the chance to do the work in national politics we'd dreamed of. I wanted to put all my energy into transforming the SDP's platform, attracting new people to the progressive movement, and creating new ways of doing politics.

However, I quickly learned that what happens inside the parliament building isn't always noble. Everything I've learned about the political game I learned from the SDP parliamentary group, and those first years were particularly grueling. They were mentally the most difficult years I'd experienced until that point, and not because of the work itself. The atmosphere could be merciless.

In retrospect I would say that my first disappointments were typical of young people in new jobs. I had expected my position in the party and success in the elections would mean I would be assigned to parliamentary committees that dealt with matters I was most interested in: economy, climate, and energy. I didn't expect to be given particularly competitive assignments, like foreign affairs or finance, or have unrealistic hopes of chairing committees or other positions with extra perks, but I did expect I'd be able to work on the things I was passionate about. Instead, as a newcomer, I was assigned to the legal affairs committee and the grand committee, which handles EU affairs. I would come to appreciate the work and make friendships that would help me, but initially I did have a bit of a wake-up call.

The other obstacles I experienced were more interpersonal. Because we're a large party, the SDP and our parliamentary group have a long history of dividing ourselves into cliques. These are mostly based on divergent views on certain issues, but they can also be based on personalities. I tried to tread lightly; I wanted to avoid taking sides and focus on the issues that had inspired me to join the party in the first place. This may sound honorable, but it was a fatal mistake. Trying to stay above the fray and outside of factions when you're seen as a rising figure who might compete for leadership in the future can make you weak. You need a solid foundation of alliances in order to get things done. In politics, people are constantly fighting for power—both outside and within their own party. It can even be easier to develop friendships outside your own group, with people you don't have to compete with.

My naiveté made me an easy target. I don't mind when people are tough in the context of getting things done—if they demand a lot, or are hard on you, that's just part of a high-intensity work environment, especially one like politics, which involves constant negotiation, debate, and compromise. But it troubled me when colleagues were rude, or cruel, in order to make me and others feel weak and hinder our ability to work effectively. Spreading gossip, including to journalists, was quite common, and the rumors often focused on accusing a person of doing something that had harmed or weakened the party, or exaggerating a mistake made during parliamentary work. There was often a sexist undertone: it was implied that women were not being team players, or just wanted attention. While most of the politicians I've worked with are genuine, warmhearted people who have chosen a career in politics because they want to change the world for the better, some will do anything to get what they want.

It was exhausting to have to constantly fight for my space. For a while, these detractors succeeded in discouraging me; the spark in me that wanted to change the world started to dim. But I knew that this was a sink-or-swim moment, and I had to adapt. The only way to cope with that environment was to be strong enough not to be pushed around. For that, I needed allies.

There was a group, mostly women, who had been politically marginalized after the former party leader, Jutta Urpilainen, lost her presidency. They were ready to show their strength by gathering a majority within the parliamentary group, and for that they needed us newcomers. Because I was working with the leader who replaced her, I wasn't welcomed with open arms. I had to prove I could be trusted, and that took time. But because I was consistent when defending our positions on different issues, I was ultimately able to develop strong relationships with these women, and they ended up supporting me for years, all the way to being elected as prime minister and after.

I'm grateful for learning these lessons early in my career, and I'm thankful for the people who helped me get through it and emerge as a tougher, more confident, and more resilient politician. I have often joked that if you can survive our parliamentary group, you can survive anything.

○

I had strengths as a politician, but I also had weaknesses. One of these was—and still is—that I'm not naturally socially talented. I am a good speaker, I'm outgoing, but I have always been first and foremost issue-oriented. I haven't cared much what people think about me, or focused on what motivates others, and I rarely have had the energy or desire to socialize with colleagues outside of work. For a long time, I remained attached to my idealistic belief that the best argument would always win in the end, and that people could be persuaded using only reason. I ignored other things that might motivate people to develop their beliefs: their goals, their feelings, and their need to be seen and valued as individuals. It's not natural to me to walk through the office asking people how they're doing, or to discuss how I felt about certain meetings or negotiations after the meetings conclude. To me, when we are done, we are done. But I quickly learned that the emotional atmosphere of a meeting could affect everything that came after. In neglecting emotions, I was making my work as a politician much harder for myself.

I learned I needed to develop different skills, like becoming more emotionally intelligent, in order to be more effective as a politician. Complicated group dynamics taught me how important it is to find allies and people you can trust, and you can't build these relationships without really connecting with others. Loyalty is more important in politics than in many other areas of society; you need to have close colleagues with whom you can talk about sensitive information and trust that they won't use it to undermine you or your arguments in meetings later. Developing these friendships helped me learn to be more sensitive in the way I interacted both in and after meetings.

I started to pay more attention to the sidelines and nuances. Up to that point, my life had been mostly work—learning about and focusing on different policies that I wanted to change. I realized this wasn't enough—I had to give my heart to politics, not just my mind.

○

Another element that took getting used to was the commute. Before I was elected to parliament, I lived with Markus in Tampere. Once I had to be in Helsinki for work, I began to split my time, renting a small studio apartment in Helsinki and coming back to Tampere most weekends and whenever parliament wasn't in session. In the Finnish parliament, Mondays are dedicated to work in your constituency, and to municipal duties, so I spent every Monday in Tampere in meetings. Despite the distance, Markus and I were very close—we would talk on the phone for hours about life, work, and everything else. At that point we had been together over ten years. We finished each other's sentences, and it was like we shared one mind. Sometimes one of us would take the two-hour train ride just to have the opportunity to sleep side by side for a night, even though it meant waking up at 5 a.m. the next morning to make it back to our respective workplaces on time. We knew the schedule was temporary, even if we didn't know exactly where I'd go next.

In 2017, just as I was adjusting to the schedule in parliament, I was faced with another choice: I could run for mayor of Tampere. While

I was still chairing the city council, my daily work was in parliament. If I wanted to try to become the mayor, it would mean giving up my work in national politics and committing full-time leading my home city. Being a mayor is a highly respected and powerful position, and much better paid than being a parliamentarian. On some level, the position, and timing, seemed fated. I was writing my master's thesis about political leadership in Finland's municipalities—specifically about the role of mayors. I had been slowly working on my master's degree since I finished my bachelor's in 2012, and after spending ten years in university I was almost done. Because I was always working, I never had time to study. (Markus jokes that I went to university about once a year, though this isn't unusual for young parliamentarians; a good friend in parliament was in the same situation.) After conducting interviews with mayors and other political officials around the country, I was finalizing my thesis—and thinking of becoming mayor myself. The job was exactly what I'd studied, and it came with the bonus of living in Tampere with Markus full-time.

Political parties usually nominate their candidates for mayor before the municipal elections, because it offers an advantage in campaigning, but officially the mayor is elected by the city council afterward. The custom has been that the party who wins the most votes in the municipal elections will get the mayor's position and the second biggest party the chair of the council. Regardless of the mayor job, it was evident that I would run to be a member of the city council again that year. I was truly interested in the work, and I felt a deep responsibility to the party. But even though in many ways it seemed like a great role for me, I didn't want to commit to being mayor. Our party agreed that we wouldn't nominate any single person to the job beforehand.

I was able to put off the decision, but the race was close and we won. Because I received the most votes of all our candidates, the party asked if I would be interested in taking on the role.

The decision was extremely hard for me, and I went back and forth many times. I made a list of pros and cons and tried to look at the situation from every angle. Was I ready to leave national politics and my work in parliament, which I'd wanted for so long? At the same time it was an incredible opportunity to lead a big city, and I was confident that I would love the job and be good at it.

Within a week, I finished my thesis and decided not to take the mayor position. Ultimately the decision came from my heart. I wasn't ready to leave national politics: I still wanted to work on our party's platform reform, especially given the possibility that we could win the next parliamentary elections in two years. I knew that if we won, I had a good chance of becoming a minister.

○

In 2017 the SDP was headed to another party congress and held elections for party leadership. Antti Rinne was elected to continue as a chair and there was also competition for the secretary general of the party and other high positions. I was elected as first vice chair, and Antton Rönnholm was elected secretary general. He was adamant about renewing the party platform that was so crucially needed, and at this moment all the conceptualizing and strategizing we'd done over the previous decade began to fall into place. We were ready to update the party for its new phase.

The first step was to set up working groups in different political fields. In total, about five hundred people in the party participated, of all ages and levels of experience. The aim was to reform our political goals and come up with concrete measures on how to achieve them. We weren't only looking at the upcoming elections and four years after that, but thinking about the targets we should have for the upcoming decade, and beyond.

I represented party leadership in our climate, energy, and environment working groups, and I participated in discussions on human rights and the rights of minority groups as well. In the end the party leadership was going to go through all the papers that the working groups created and develop an election program based on this work, but I wanted to be active in the preliminary work as well. I wanted to make sure we were ambitious and brave with our proposals.

Rönnholm had a strong vision for how to organize the work. It was important that as many people as possible could participate and feel part of creating the program. More and more people became invested in the party's success because they felt the party represented their actual views, and because they were proud to be associated with it. The path to creating our policies was as important, or even more important, than the outcome. At its best, politics gives people the power to imagine the future, and we were asking an important question. What should our society look like in 2030, and what reforms would we need to get there? Our guidance was simple: be bold in your vision, don't hold back.

Ultimately, we wanted the platform to acknowledge the party's history of fighting for labor rights and social welfare while updating those positions for the twenty-first century. We wanted to create a program that had elements of sustainability at its core: social justice and economic welfare, within the boundaries of the planet. These reforms were practical and local, but they also responded to the undeniable facts of the major challenges that humankind is facing. The threat of climate catastrophe couldn't be pushed aside anymore. We set very progressive goals for revitalizing Finland's parental leave system and advocating for fair conditions in working life. We wanted healthcare reforms, and especially reforms on eldercare so that people could feel confident they would grow old with dignity. The education reforms that included mandatory schooling until age eighteen, and free books and tools for all secondary school students, were part of these proposals as well. We also set out to enhance the rights of every citizen, focusing especially on strengthening the right to self-determination for transgender people, as well as to bolster the rights of Sami people, the indigenous population that lives in the north of the country. We wanted to set a target for Finland to be climate neutral by 2035, and net negative soon after that. And we had progressive views on the economy as well, on how we should change our taxation system and boost sustainable growth and employment.

This was the moment I and many others had been waiting for. It felt like we were making history. This was how we would attempt to win the next elections, and it would form the core of the next government's agenda if we succeeded. As we debated, agreed, disagreed, and compromised, it felt like we had finally reached the end of a period of stagnation and the beginning of a new phase. We weren't only writing a program, but actually strengthening our party's self-esteem. People not only felt that we could win—they began to feel that it was vital that we did.

Politics is too often seen as a game of power, and in many ways, it is. But it's also so much more than that. People join movements because they want to change the world and influence the future. The things that they want to change might be big or small, but it's the issues that drive them. This is the substance that helps a movement either grow or wither over time. Politics isn't about just tactics and strategy but about passion, values, and ideology. It's a combination of different types of people and views, and it works best when the system allows these different people to find consensus and compromise on behalf of something bigger.

○

By the time we began to reform our party platform, my schedule was packed. I was so glad I had finished my master's degree that spring, so one weight was off my shoulders, but I still had work in parliament, in the party, and in local politics in Tampere. Plus, I was aware that I was getting older, and some of my friends who had tried to get pregnant were dealing with fertility issues. I knew that I wanted to have at least one child—maybe more. I'd always imagined myself as a mom at some point, but I'd never felt any rush. Markus and I got engaged in 2016, and we had discussed our future and having children, but the timing never seemed right. There was always so much going on professionally; like many working couples, we postponed all personal matters for a hazy, unforeseeable future.

That year was no different: the timing didn't feel right. But I started to realize that the timing probably would never feel right while I was working in politics, and I began to worry that the problems that our friends were facing might happen to us. So Markus and I agreed to try for a baby, thinking that if it happened, it happened.

It turned out to be the best choice I've ever made, and the timing was better than I could have anticipated. In January 2018, I gave birth to our daughter, Emma. Markus and I had discussed all the things that we would have to figure out once our child was born, and there were two things that were especially important to me: first, that we split parental leave so that both of us could equally participate in both work and family life, and second, that our child would have my last name. The name was easy, but Markus needed more convincing on the question of equal parental leave. He worked as an entrepreneur, and for him it was both a matter of how to organize his work and facing a decline in income. As a parliamentarian, I could have spent an entire year at home with full pay. But it was a matter of principle to me, as well as a practical one. I wanted to return to my political work well before we headed into the election.

So we agreed to split leave evenly: six months for me, six months for Markus. I really enjoyed staying at home with Emma. I love being a mom, and Emma was a healthy and happy baby. Markus has said many times since then that he is grateful that he got to spend so much time with her as a baby because it created a tight bond between them and gave him confidence as a parent.

○

After six months of leave, I went back to parliament, and by the time the next parliamentary elections came around at the beginning of 2019, the SDP were leading the discussion on many core issues, in no small part because of our new platform. It was the first moment in my lifetime that I'd ever felt we were at the forefront of the political discourse, and it was because we were focused not on how to keep things the way they were, but on how to change things and prepare for a future that would be better for everyone. It was too soon to tell, but it seemed that all our hard work might lead us to victory.

You already know what happened next. Rinne got sick, and when it fell to me to lead the election campaign in his absence, I was daunted. I was only serving my first term in parliament, and I'd just returned from parental leave with a one-year-old baby at home. But I had also been advocating for the party platform reform since I was part of the youth movement in the late 2000s, and I knew it inside and out. For this reason I believed I could effectively campaign in Rinne's stead while he recovered. And I wanted to show that I was up to the task even if it intimidated me.

Though Rinne was absent for several weeks of the campaign, and still weak from his treatment when he returned, we won. We negotiated a new government program based on our ideas and our party's new vision. Rinne had strong values and views on what we needed to reform—I think it was why he and I always got along well. His background in labor unions meant he was very good at negotiating and organizing, and at creating platforms for other people to lead. When I got the offer from Rinne to become minister of transportation and communications, there was never a question whether I would take it. It was a chance to show that I could lead a ministry, and to have more influence and power.

Our population is small, but Finland is a big country in terms of land mass. Members of parliament from remote districts would fly home from Helsinki, and in the winter it's never a given that the weather will cooperate with the parliamentary schedule. Usually, people are in Helsinki four days a week, with Monday set aside for work in your region and connecting with constituents.

When Markus was on parental leave, he often took care of Emma in our small studio apartment that I had rented near our party's headquarters in Helsinki my first parliamentary term. I took every opportunity to rush home to see them and breastfeed Emma during the workdays. By the time I became a minister in 2019, Emma was in daycare. She and Markus lived in Tampere while I commuted back and forth, which meant she was near her grandparents—Markus's parents and my mother both lived very close to us. This strong support network made it easier to balance my job with motherhood. I was still working a lot by any standard, but I didn't feel like it because I enjoyed the work so much and could count on everything being okay at home. Because of Finland's strong social safety net and my family's support, there was never a question that I'd be able to pursue a high-level career in politics. But for a single parent without the help from close family, this would have been so much harder, if not impossible.

Although female politicians face unique challenges when attempting to balance work and home life, it's also true that the job isn't what it used to be for anyone. Being a politician is no longer valued the way it once was, and there are many reasons for that. The pace and number of issues have grown significantly, so you always feel you're underperforming—voters often agree—while compensation is lower relative to salaries in the private sector than it used to be. Politicians face constant scrutiny, and the rise of social media has made hate speech a daily reality. The ever-growing competition for readers' attention and advertising money in the traditional press has made polarizing stories the norm rather than the exception. Once you leave politics, it might be hard to find a job outside it, and that's a reality you have to face every time there's an election, when voters might decide to replace you. Members of parliament who come from business or other industries are usually shocked at the amount of work and what it demands of you. The sheer number of different interest groups and stakeholders is overwhelming on its own, and the environment can be quite brutal sometimes. It's a difficult career.

So why do it? It isn't exactly a normal working life, but when you're a politician, you know that whatever difficulty you might be going through in your work isn't going to last forever. It's a four-year term, and during that term, you have a mission. It isn't that that mission is "bigger" than your family, but not everyone can be a politician, and it's a great honor to be elected and be able to influence matters that affect everyone. I have said this out loud many times because I see nothing wrong with admitting that I wanted power. Women are often encouraged to hide their ambitions, and to be coy, or modest, about their aspirations. But this only holds us back. I never saw a reason to pretend I wasn't motivated by power when everyone knows that power is the fuel in the engine that is politics. I wanted to do and change things, and for that I needed the same thing men have no problem admitting they want.

○

Although I was a minister for only a short time—around six months—before I became prime minister, it was a crucial period of growth for me. I don't think I could have effectively taken the lead as prime minister without this experience. I learned how to lead the ministry and how to push major projects and legislation forward.

Every position and experience I have taken has taught me not only something specific about that field, but most importantly, that when we feel unprepared is a time we can learn the most. The tasks that are intimidating and challenging help us grow. These are the ones we should embrace, especially when we feel uncomfortable and don't know what lies ahead. Knowledge is important, but willingness to learn is even more so.

Like many people, I can be intimidated by new things. When I was younger, public speaking scared the hell out of me. I always blushed throughout, and because of that, I became very self-conscious and afraid of it. But I didn't let that discourage me. Instead, I decided that I would practice speaking in public as often as I could, so I would train myself not to feel so uncomfortable anymore. After a while, speaking in public became natural and comfortable for me—and eventually my blushing faded, too. Often, diligent practicing shows us that the task we were so afraid of is something we can do. The unrealistic expectations we have for ourselves are our biggest obstacles, and accepting that we are never ready can help us evolve. We learn by doing.

Once we formed our government and were able to begin work, it was a very inspiring, optimistic time. The entire government was based on the idea of sustainable development—socially, economically, and environmentally—and we had many big, progressive reforms planned. One thing that we wanted to start working on right away was our climate targets, and as the minister of transport and communications I was working on these issues. Although I'd initially hoped to become the minister for climate, it turned out many things landed on my desk that made an even greater impact on our emissions and net zero goal.

One part of our progressive agenda was to boost the overall investments in transportation and improve the condition of our infrastructure network. Because Finland is not a small country, in terms of area, we have a lot of roads, railroads, and waterways to maintain and improve. I was fortunate to have a large budget for this, and the biggest investments that were made in the beginning of our government were under my remit.

The Ministry for Transport and Communication was well organized, and we had weekly meetings on all the issues that needed my view and approval as a minister. Three of the biggest projects we focused on were infrastructure plans for our railways, fixing taxi legislation, and creating a parliamentary system for how to plan and execute major national infrastructure needs in the future; we also had to negotiate development agreements between the national government and the country's biggest cities that included transportation, housing, and land use. The team and I went through files of information every week so that nothing would go unnoticed. I wanted to be thorough and brought huge binders, often containing several hundred pages, to these meetings. I was in charge of liaising on EU-wide transportation and communication legislation as well.

Although it wasn't as pressing an issue as it is now, artificial intelligence was an emerging theme. That was particularly interesting, and thorny, because it was totally new: many of the questions about the ethics of AI and other new technologies had only been asked in theory, and now the technology was knocking at the door. Data use and protecting the rights of EU citizens were a constant concern, as was the security of our data networks. We met several times to discuss the reliability of the Chinese telecommunications company Huawei and who could control critically important networks. Public officials in our ministry favored a market-based approach, but I was looking at this also from the perspective of security, as were officials from ministries that dealt with foreign and security issues. Representatives from the Chinese embassy and Huawei wanted to meet with me; at the time, China had engaged with more aggressive foreign policy toward some European countries, and their officials were very sensitive to anything negative concerning their interests. As in many issues, it was a matter of balancing between different views and trying to tackle multiple angles. I was as diplomatic as I could be, but made sure that security remained on the table when we evaluated our legislation on the matter.

Normally, the minister for transportation and communications isn't in the spotlight as much as I was. But because we had reworked the party platform, we were very ambitious, and the scale of the projects that fell under my mandate meant it was important that I constantly engage with the public. I realized the years I'd spent doing televised debates and traveling the country giving speeches had prepared me well for a role that required many press conferences and interviews. It's important to be willing to take chances and try new things in any job you have; sometimes you don't realize until after the fact that you've been preparing for the next step.

In October 2019, I traveled with the President of the Republic of Finland Sauli Niinistö, and his delegation to the White House to meet with President Trump. President Niinistö only traveled with ministers if there was a specific reason for us to accompany him, and I was there to negotiate and offer input on a major transportation issue on the agenda. All and all it was an unforgettable visit. I stayed in the White House guesthouse, a beautiful, historic building, with my state secretary and the other members of the Finnish delegation. In short breaks between meetings, Markus sent me photos and videos of Emma, who had already learned to say some words.

I remember feeling anxious because President Trump was (and is) an unpredictable personality, and I was worried how he would react to me as a thirty-three-year-old woman working in government. Would he be professional, or would he overlook me? I remember being worried about the possibility of a meeting becoming awkward or uncomfortable. The United States is a crucially important partner to Finland, and I didn't want to unwittingly contribute to any diplomatic difficulties.

The discussion took place over lunch, and we sat across from each other—the presidents sat in the middle, and I was at our president's right side. Sometimes when I mention I had a meeting over lunch with President Trump, people ask me what he ate. I am not sure that I remember, but I do know he drank a Coke with his meal. The issue we discussed was that the United States needed new ships that could operate in frozen waters during the winter—colloquially known as icebreakers—and they wanted to buy or rent some of ours.

In Finland, modesty is very important, and pride is considered suspicious. However, I am comfortable saying that Finland makes the world's best icebreakers. Furthermore, our icebreakers use more green and innovative technologies. There is a very practical reason for our superiority: all of our ports are frozen during winter, and as a geographically isolated part of Europe, we need our sea routes for shipping. We need icebreakers to ensure that our imports and exports can move through our harbors throughout the year, and we have designed about 80 percent of the world's icebreakers.

You can't enter the northern seas, with either civilian or military vessels, if you don't have an icebreaker, and because tensions with Russia and China were deepening at the time of this meeting, this discussion was not just about the ability to operate in freezing waters. In the years since, China and Russia have agreed to cooperate to create new trade and military routes through the Arctic, and Russia has a fleet of about forty ice-breaking ships—by far the largest in the world. China also has a fleet, mostly grown in the last five years. This development has given NATO and the rest of Europe major reservations, as it could lead to Russia becoming the main supplier of a technology that will shape geopolitics and control crucial trade routes in the coming years. At the time of the meeting with President Trump, the United States had only two functioning icebreakers that could operate in polar waters, the *Polar Star* and the *Healy*, and they weren't in good shape. One article from the time referred to the imbalance between their capabilities and Russia and China's as the "icebreaker gap."

Finland wanted to build and sell these ships to the US, and President Trump wanted to buy them, because they were better and much less expensive than those the US could manufacture. Unfortunately, it's not so simple for the United States to purchase Finnish icebreakers. They couldn't just place an order with us. In the United States, there is a great deal of regulation that determines that critical equipment like ships need to be produced in the US. For example, the Jones Act, established in 1920, requires that all cargo vessels traveling between two US ports must be built in the United States. It also requires that these vessels be owned and registered by US entities, and that they be operated by US crews. The legislation's initial purpose was to ensure the United States maintained the capacity to build ships at all times, to be prepared for war or emergencies. But in the globalized economy, the result has been more or less the opposite: they have diminished capacity in some areas.

So when I met with President Trump, we had to discuss how to get around these restrictions. One idea was that the US could build their own icebreakers with Finnish assistance. But it would cost the country much, much more to set up the infrastructure to produce icebreakers at the level that Finland does, and it was likely that the ships wouldn't be as good as those produced in Finland.

Another idea was that the United States could lease some of our ships to make sure they wouldn't be left at a disadvantage compared to Russia and China. But Finland needed our own icebreakers. Sometimes we don't need every single icebreaker, depending on the weather conditions—but that is unpredictable, and some winters we need all the capacity we have.

Even though that meeting didn't end with the purchase of Finnish icebreakers, we agreed to continue cooperating on the issue and to map out how Finnish companies and experts could help the US tackle this problem. In 2024, the US, Canada, and Finland signed the Ice Pact agreement that enables the countries to produce a fleet of polar icebreaker ships together. It is a significant step forward to make sure NATO countries have the ability to operate in the Arctic Ocean that will become more and more important in the future.

I was relieved that the meeting and discussion went without issue. It wasn't until later that things took a turn. The presidents held a press conference in which Trump bashed his political opponents on issues that had nothing to do with the visit, and at the end of the conference he walked out of the room leaving Niinistö behind, looking a bit puzzled at the podium.

# 5.

# BECOMING A "FEMALE LEADER"

**It was lucky that Markus and I** had developed a good rhythm with child-care before the sudden elections that made me prime minister. There was no adjustment period. Because this election had taken place during the previous prime minister's term, I had to pick up right where Rinne left off. As my team balanced the onslaught of inter-view requests, and dodged photographers waiting outside meetings, hoping to get a shot of the new leader, the cabinet had our work cut out for us. Although I was young when I was elected, I wasn't inexperienced—I had enough experience to know that I had no idea what was in store for me.

The image of Finland that circulated in the international press—as a kind of egalitarian, feminist paradise, albeit one with harsh winters—would prove hard to live up to. Of course, Finnish society has problems, and it is not as if having a female leader is a surefire way to solve everything. Moreover, I did not, and still do not, think of myself as a "female leader." I think of myself as a person entrusted to lead, and as a representative of a movement that includes better rights for women and minorities among a slate of progressive values. As prime minister, I hoped to use my leadership and negotiating skills, and my experience in politics and government, to advance those values. My party was relying on me to continue work on the government program we'd set when Antti Rinne took office. Even though the prime minister changed, it was important that the party goals remained in sight, and that we didn't lose sight of the movement. And I had to start right away.

I was elected to be the candidate on Sunday night. On Monday, I met with the leaders of all the different parties in government to negotiate two things: first, to confirm the continuation of our governmental program, and second, to get their guarantee that they would support me in parliament when it met to officially elect the prime minister. On Tuesday, the tenth of December, parliament convened to vote. Because I was in parliament when I was elected, I sat in my regular seat during the vote, next to one of my best friends, Ilmari Nurminen, one of the people who had gathered in my apartment to celebrate after the vote in our party council. In the photos from the moment they declared I'd won the parliamentary vote, you can see my shock had not quite worn off yet. I went to the Presidential Palace, where President Niinistö officially granted resignation to the old government and appointed me and my government in front of the media. On Wednesday, I chaired a meeting of our ministerial committee on EU affairs—part of the prime minister's mandate—where we determined Finland's positions on issues at the final meeting of the year of the European Council and attended a mandatory hearing in the parliament's EU committee on the meeting scheduled for the next day. On Thursday, I flew to the European Council meeting in Brussels. Finland still held the rotating presidency, so the next day I held a press conference together with Charles Michel, the president of the European Council, and Ursula von der Leyen, the president of the European Commission. Two of Finland's top priorities for our term were ambitious climate policy and strengthening the rule of law—one of the fundamental principles of the EU, which establishes that all member states follow the same EU law and abide by clear democratic principles like equality before the law and independent courts—and we conducted negotiations to set a target of net-zero carbon emissions for the EU by 2050 and make abiding by the rule of law a requirement for access to funds from the European budget.

On Friday, I flew back to Finland, and to Tampere, where Markus and Emma were waiting for me. As soon as I got home, she ran up to me and ripped at my shirt; I was still breastfeeding her at the time. Looking back, I have no idea how I managed to work such long hours and commute a few times a week between Tampere and Helsinki, and still breastfeed occasionally. But that weekend I stayed home with my family and relaxed. We went to the Christmas market and prepared for the holidays that were just a week away.

○

Meanwhile, the problems I had inherited were not entry-level issues for a new leader, and they immediately required our full attention.

To start, there were a couple of major national issues that needed a firm hand to steer. As transportation minister, I had already been dealing with the disastrous effects of new legislation on taxi services that had been passed in 2017. While Finland has a relatively small population of about 5.5 million, it is geographically larger, about the size of Montana. Much of the country is sparsely populated, and people who don't live in cities often need to cover long distances to reach schools, hospitals, and other basic services. This creates certain challenges for the country's infrastructure, particularly transportation. For a long time, we had legislation that addressed this population distribution: taxi services operated in every region, even places where operating taxis was not as profitable. You could call a taxi anywhere in the country, and prices were regulated so that people who lived far from population centers didn't have to pay more to access services. Long after rideshare apps had become the standard in much of the world, Finland still didn't recognize Uber. Maintaining this regulatory atmosphere was essential to ensuring every Finnish citizen could live and work. In many areas, taxi services were even used to take children to school.

But after the elections in 2015, the center-right-wing coalition decided to switch to the free market–based app model that was spreading across the West, permitting Uber and other rideshare apps to operate in the country. Everyone knew this would cause problems. Neither drivers nor the majority of citizens wanted it. When it took effect, in

July 2018; the change was dramatic. Traditional taxi operators stopped serving in many rural areas, and attempting to call a taxi from these regions meant long wait times and higher, often prohibitive, prices. Because there was no market incentive to operate a taxi in remote areas, people without cars, or who could not drive, were often stuck with very limited transportation options available. Rideshare operators for apps like Uber became concentrated in urban areas, but even in cities, getting a ride became a stressful, uncertain prospect.

When the Social Democrats took office in 2019, we wanted to repair some of the damage caused by this legislation. Indeed, I believe the taxi law is one of the reasons the center-right coalition support dived the year before, which helped the Social Democrats win the elections. But it is much easier to initiate a deregulatory change than to revert to stricter regulations. Attempts at regulating the new market for taxis and rideshares have proven nightmarish: many former professional drivers have left the field, unable to earn a good salary on piecemeal gig-economy work. What's more, the EU framework made it hard to transition back to the highly regulated model we had before. And even after years of fixing problems in the legislation, no minister or government has been able to truly repair the situation.

○

Another issue that we had to deal with was the country's ongoing problems around eldercare. There had been a huge scandal around widespread neglect and mistreatment of residents of assisted-living facilities and nursing homes. In January 2019, investigations found that a lack of qualified staff had led to the improper handling of medications and severe neglect of elderly residents, many of whom had been underfed, not taken outside often enough, and left to sleep in unsanitary conditions. After a resident's death at one nursing home was suspected to have been caused by malpractice, the facility was shut down. The CEO of two of the largest operators of assisted-living facilities in the country resigned.

This issue was very important to me and to our party. One of our biggest promises in the initial parliamentary elections that year was to take care of this inhumane situation by, among other changes, increasing the eldercare workforce. As in many Western countries, Finland has an aging population and needs more people working in the social and healthcare sector. To find the personnel to do this difficult work, we would have to educate more workers, attract employees who have left the field to come back to work, and bring in suitable people from abroad and train them. These jobs are not entry-level—they require training, and come with a lot of responsibility, and the government would have to provide programs and funding to bring in more workers with the necessary skills.

Because of the urgency of the crisis, as well as the knowledge that it would be hard to tackle both in legislation and concretely on the ground, we knew we had to find the money fast—over 200 million euros—to start the long process of reforming this sector. For months, attempts to secure funding for this initiative were stalled, which was very frustrating. We had negotiated the objective itself in the governmental program, but part of the funding had remained an open question, and now it couldn't wait any longer. Once I took office, we started the negotiations with four other coalition parties on how to finance the reform, but it was difficult. There was resistance, particularly from the Center Party, who were in charge of the Ministry of Finance. They knew reforming the eldercare system had been one of our top priorities, and that our party had made a political mistake not to secure enough money in the negotiations six months earlier. For me, it was the first real test of my ability to lead in a high-stakes situation. If I had lost this battle, I would have seemed weak, which could have affected my entire term in office. And I felt the pressure.

Since the original mistake was ours and not much time had passed since the initial negotiations, we didn't have much leverage. So we had to find the money under the budget of our own minister in the field of social services and healthcare, and from targets that were equally important to us. We also had to prepare the proposal in a way that would be acceptable to other parties, who took full advantage of our self-made problem. We came to the negotiating table again and again with new solutions only to hear the words "this won't work for us." The negotiations lasted the entire month of January, but eventually we were able to secure the funding. I was relieved—our number one promise to our voters would finally progress.

○

But the most pressing problem that I dealt with when I arrived was an international situation that had been lingering all fall. Around ten mothers and thirty children who were Finnish citizens had ended up in the al-Hol displaced persons camp in northern Syria, near the border with Iraq. A series of anti-ISIS battles in late 2018 and early 2019 had filled the camp with the wives and children of men suspected of collaborating with the terrorist organization. The camp was controlled by forces associated with the Western-backed Syrian Democratic Forces, who were fighting against Syrian nationalist and Islamist forces, and al-Hol went from housing around 9,500 people to more than 70,000 people within about six months. The conditions in the camp were inhumane: people there lacked food, clean water, and access to basic services and infrastructure, and because all residents there are assumed to have ISIS affiliations—though not all of them necessarily do—the security situation is so extreme that it is still often referred to as a prison camp in a de facto war zone.

I had had strong opinions on what Finland should do about our citizens in al-Hol since the situation arose the previous year. When the Social Democrats won the parliamentary election that spring, I was vocal about my view in meetings and government discussions. We needed to respect the children's rights, protect their lives, and bring them back to Finland. The mothers were adults who had made their own decisions, and many could be suspected of collaborating with ISIS voluntarily, but the children were being denied basic human rights every minute they remained in the camp. Their welfare was our country's responsibility. If we could not legally separate the children from their parents, then their parents would have to come back to Finland, too. It was crystal-clear to me that bringing the children back was our obligation according to the UN's Convention on the Rights of the Child, and that there should be no more discussion on whether we "should" do it. We had to.

Although I was not the only person who had clarity on this issue, the process of repatriating these children was not simple, and the question of what to do about them had been hovering over Antti Rinne's government all fall, for both ideological and logistical reasons.

Politically, the children's parents were seen as potential terrorists, and many people believed that allowing them to return to Finland would constitute a security threat. We had no legal grounds or tools to separate the children from their families, so as discussions continued, it became evident that if we were to embark on repatriation, we would have to bring the mothers, too. My stance was the same: if there was no other way to help the children, then we should bring them back with their mothers. But even discussing the fate of the children was controversial. While the mothers were seen as potential terrorists, some also feared the children would have been radicalized by their parents and the atmosphere of the camp while living there. The children were of all ages, from babies born in the camp to prepubescent girls forced to marry old men. To me, the suggestion that these girls were "terrorists" was absurd—as if it was their fault they had been forced to marry. For years, the biggest terrorism threat in Finland had been militant right-wing forces, which were much more difficult for Finnish security services to manage than it would be for them to monitor a handful of women and their children. But the narrative that we would be welcoming terrorists into our country persisted.

Logistically, the process of extracting our citizens from the camp was not as simple as showing up on a chartered flight and collecting them. First, we had to locate our citizens and contact them on the ground, which was a difficult task in itself. Then we had to persuade the mothers to let their children return to Finland with or without them, and negotiate with the people who ran the camp. While the camp was technically overseen by US-backed forces, control was divided among different armed groups. There was no official government with whom to discuss the removal and repatriation of these people. We also knew that problems wouldn't end with the extraction of the children from the camp. After they returned to Finland, both children and mothers would face stigma that would make it difficult for them to reintegrate into our society. It was likely the children would be taken away from their mothers, for their own safety and well-being, and all these people would have to be monitored by social workers and security officials.

Antti Rinne's administration had struggled to make progress on the issue and was divided: the problem was seen as conflict between children's rights and security. We had discussed the matter for months in different ways, and the foreign minister Pekka Haavisto was trying to find a solution. He needed the support for his plan to appoint a special envoy to negotiate and retrieve citizens from the camp, but Rinne hesitated taking a leading role and responsibility for possibly flammable political consequences. So we were stuck still discussing the issue when we really should have made a decision about it a long time ago. This had severe repercussions—Haavisto's attempts to move ahead with his ministerial authority, and through the Ministry for Foreign Affairs, ended in a yearlong hearing in parliament's constitutional committee, and he was torn apart by the media and rival politicians. I always thought this was unfair, and I urged him not to let these people pressure him to resign and allow it to determine his career and legacy.

So when I started my work as prime minister, al-Hol was among the first things on my agenda. Negotiations began within a week of my taking office. Far from causing the high-stakes deadlock that it had created previously, the solution was reached in a single day. It only took the will and courage to make a decision. We were able to agree that the government would do everything we could to repatriate the children. After the negotiations, we held a press conference and announced that Finland would begin the process.

Other European countries had been struggling with the same deadlock on this issue that we had, and as soon as we announced our plan, it set a precedent that other countries could follow. Still, politicians have been reluctant and slow to solve the issue completely, and the camp is still running.

Even after our very clear decision, it was difficult to execute. The mothers had to agree to come back to Finland voluntarily, and some of them wouldn't. A few families came willingly. A few months later, another decided to come. Then, a few months later, another would decide to come. While the government had unilaterally agreed to bring the children back, much of the decision-making about their lives in Finland had to be handled by social workers and other public officials, who would decide if they could remain with their parents once in the country or if they would have to be cared for by other relatives, like grandparents who were also Finnish citizens. The process dragged on—which was why it was so important that we initiated it as soon as possible.

Once again, I came to realize that in the most complex situations you should always lean on your values, even if it might feel uncomfortable at first. The more time you spend lingering on an issue, the harder it will be to make a decision. Even in the most difficult situations, your values can be the anchor that keeps you grounded in a world that is often complex and unclear. If you do what you know deep down in your heart is right, you can stand up straight even when you face headwinds. And that feeling is powerful.

○

My first month in office was no gentle on-ramp. By the time I participated in the World Economic Forum in Davos near the end of January 2020, I had completely revised my understanding of what it means to lead and to govern. Day by day, I became less shocked and overwhelmed by my new responsibilities simply because I had no time to dwell. I had handled the challenges I faced as soon as I won the election the best I could, and every day that passed I gained more experience and understanding that would help me serve in the role.

I do not think feeling unprepared to lead a country is an unusual experience for world leaders, no matter their age (and certainly no matter their gender). Nevertheless, my age and gender remained a persistent issue for journalists and even colleagues at the WEF, which was one of the first times I could see the effects of the extraordinary media attention I'd received since I won the election the month before. Even as I gave interviews on Finland's ambitious climate goals and sat on a panel with Al Gore to discuss climate change, I was constantly being asked some version of the same question, which I felt was irrelevant given the work I was there to do: "How does it feel to be a prime minister when you're so young, and a woman?" In another panel one journalist even asked me, "How does it work" when five of a country's parliamentary leaders are women?

The question baffled me. The implication was that women must have a radically different way of governing that might totally derail the government. But we had just concluded extremely difficult negotiations on eldercare and made huge progress on repatriating children from a notoriously dangerous detainment camp in Syria. It wasn't as if we met in the women's locker room, or the nail salon, to conduct these negotiations. While we may have talked about slightly different topics when we were off duty, when we were doing the work we did it the same as anyone would. It's politics, not a knitting club.

There was no time to dwell on these prejudices; there was too much to do. On top of it all, among my daily agendas, there were more and more news items about a new virus spreading in China.

# 6.

# THE PANDEMIC

**Of all the challenges I faced during my term** as a prime minister, leading a nation through a global pandemic was in many ways the most difficult. COVID-19 was an acute and quickly evolving crisis that challenged governments on all fronts. It brought the world to its knees at a time when we thought that all our advancements would have made us more prepared to prevent such a catastrophe. For decades, leaders around the world ignored scientists who warned of the possibility of a severe global pandemic. When the reality of the situation dawned on us, we were already too late.

As a leader, I experienced COVID as an exceptionally difficult and complex crisis to handle. The challenges changed as time passed and new waves of the virus emerged; what we learned in a previous phase may have helped us in some way, but new phases would create completely different problems that we hadn't foreseen. At the beginning of the pandemic, in early spring 2020, the biggest challenges were the result of a lack of knowledge and the need to make unprecedented decisions, and fast. While everyone learned how to live with the situation, it became more difficult to lead in a centralized and streamlined way. An endless stream of opinions pulled us in different directions. I am known for my clarity, but that was difficult to provide.

The first days and weeks dealing with COVID were like waking up inside a nightmare every morning. "Is this really happening?" I asked myself over and over again, getting out of bed by 6 a.m. at the latest in order to deal with all the things on my desk. The amount of information to absorb and problems to handle was so overwhelming that each day felt like a week and each week like a month. Even though we worked around the clock, we were constantly lagging behind. I still can't quite comprehend the volume of legislation we pushed through parliament during the first months of the pandemic, in addition to everything else we had to deal with.

The key players tackling COVID varied from country to country. In Finland, the government was responsible for managing the pandemic, but many other actors were involved as well. It was clear from the beginning that we would base our decisions on the most accurate research and data we had available, and that we would work closely with scientists and health authorities. But because handling the pandemic didn't only concern the healthcare sector but our society in general, the number of different ministries, industries, agencies, and organizations involved was huge. Our infectious disease legislation is structured such that actual decision-making power is distributed across several levels and among a number of institutions: the government, regional state authorities, hospital districts, and municipalities. Because we were responsible not only for treating the sick but also for preventing the disease from spreading, it meant that we had to get this whole orchestra playing the same tune. It was complicated, to put it mildly.

Despite all the difficulties, Finland also has historic and structural advantages that enabled us to cope with the situation better than many other countries. One of our greatest strengths is the deep trust that our people feel toward institutions, various authorities, and each other. When people trust that they will be taken care of throughout their lives, no matter what happens to them, and that they can be educated and participate equally in society, then they will be more likely to support what's best for the common good. When we had to lock down and advise everyone to avoid social contact, people listened to us. Without citizens' willing (and mostly voluntary) participation, we couldn't have managed to keep the infection numbers so well under control throughout the crisis. Trust like this can't be built in a few years; it takes decades to become the foundation of a society.

Nevertheless, I had just taken office, and the deluge of information, threats to health and safety, and legislative and logistical problems was unlike anything even more experienced politicians would have found easy to manage. Health authorities and the government's Situation Center had been monitoring the spread of SARS-CoV-2 since the first information about the new virus originating from Hubei province in China became public at the beginning of 2020. The government had declared COVID as a generally hazardous communicable disease on February 13, and we had made general preparations in different sectors, but at that stage the overall steering of the matter was in the hands of the Ministry of Social Affairs and Health (STM) and the Finnish Institute for Health and Welfare (THL). Before the COVID epidemic exploded into a pandemic, other matters filled the political landscape. January had been spent in those intense negotiations about funding for improvements to eldercare services. In February we were following the serious situation at the border between Turkey and Greece after President Erdoğan announced that Turkey would no longer detain migrants trying to reach Europe, going against the agreement Turkey had with the EU.

The first time I addressed COVID formally was at the end of February. A parliamentarian from our own party, Aki Lindén, a medical doctor with a long background working in healthcare organizations, including as the head of the biggest hospital in Helsinki, encouraged me to bring the topic to parliament. He had been worried about the virus from the beginning and we had discussed the matter many times. So I gave an announcement to the parliament on Finland's preparedness for the possible spread of the coronavirus. At the time, there had been fewer than five hundred cases of the disease diagnosed in Europe, most of which were in Italy; in Finland, there had been only two confirmed cases. Even if we ramped up monitoring, it was still a wait-and-see situation—following the assessments we received from the European Centre for Disease Prevention and Control (ECDC) and the World Health Organization (WHO).

A week after speaking about the issue in parliament, I went to New York to give a speech at the United Nations for International

Women's Day, where people gathered in great numbers from all over the world. After the speech at the UN I gave a guest lecture at Columbia University about sustainable development and Finland's climate policy. It's surreal to remember it now: the lecture hall was so packed with people that everyone couldn't fit into the auditorium. There were no restrictions on holding big events or travel; the Finnish media present in New York were mostly asking about the situation at the Greek border.

Just a week later the world would shut down. I returned to Finland on Saturday, March 7, and the next day I discussed COVID during the prime minister's interview hour, a traditional radio show typically broadcast approximately once a month, on a Sunday. People had seen news footage of airports carrying out random temperature checks on travelers, and I was asked whether Finland should begin implementing these measures. Our health officials didn't recommend anything like this because many infected people didn't have any symptoms and fever wouldn't show during the incubation period of the disease, so I answered that we would leave these kinds of spectacles to others and focus on measures that would have actual impact. We would be ready to discuss restrictions if there were to be an epidemic in Finland, not only individual cases. Still, many were worried. Twenty-three infections had been confirmed at the time, and people needed reassurance that we were responding seriously to the situation.

On Monday the leaders of the parliamentary parties convened to meet President Niinistö to discuss hybrid threats concerning our border and the need to update the Emergency Powers Act, because the situation in Greece was severe. COVID was also touched on, but it wasn't the main subject of the meeting.

On Tuesday morning, March 10, we gathered with the four other leaders of the government to discuss COVID and what measures we would need to take in order to avoid mass contamination in Finland. The first thing on our list was to restrict public events and large gatherings. I was particularly concerned about a possible outbreak of the virus on one of the cruise ships sailing between Finland and Estonia or Finland and Sweden. But when I asked about the possibility of stopping cruise ships, the Ministry of Transportation and Communications answered that there was not much we could do to stop private companies from operating. It was obvious that we were lacking the necessary tools to handle the developing situation and our legislation was not built to lock down public and private services on a large scale. Another thing that was alarming was the statistic that a substantial number of Finnish mobile plans were abroad at the time; many people were on ski trips in Europe and cases started bursting at these resorts. Although there hadn't been that many cases diagnosed in Finland yet, that would probably change as people traveled back home. This information was shocking, and we knew we needed to act fast and decisively if we wanted to keep the situation under control.

I had asked the COVID-19 coordination group that I had appointed in February, to prepare measures for the government to deliberate, but drafting radical unforeseen actions with tight time frames proved extremely challenging for the civil service. Until then I'd trusted the normal structure of leadership—that public officials would prepare plans for the government to debate and approve or reject—but at that moment I realized that we would need to take full political control of preparations. We didn't have time to wait for the machine to wake up to the gravity of the situation. So I asked the minister of Family Affairs and Social Services, Krista Kiuru, to draft a set of restrictions that we could approve within the next few days.

Later that same day, I participated in a videoconference for the European Council, a meeting of EU heads of state and government. The major theme was Italy: the situation there was becoming critical. Clusters of infections in the northern part of the country were already straining the health system. Two days before, fifteen provinces in the north had announced a quarantine, and that day the prime minister, Giuseppe Conte, would announce a lockdown for the entire country. The spread was quickly becoming unmanageable there, and it was likely the rest of Europe would soon follow.

After Conte finished speaking, Angela Merkel gave her thoughts, and they were unambiguous: the virus was going to be the biggest economic crisis for Europe in decades. As soon as we got off the call, I contacted the leader of one of the coalition partners—Katri Kulmuni, the minister of finance. We had to prepare for a massive economic shock, and the resources we had discussed in earlier preparation plans wouldn't be nearly enough for what was coming.

The next day, March 11, WHO declared COVID a pandemic. Our teams were rapidly making the first list of restrictions, and I checked in with Kiuru—who worked closely on the matter with another minister from STM, Aino-Kaisa Pekonen—throughout the day. As their focus was on the list with experts from the THL, mine was on the process which should involve all key institutions: the government, the parliament, and the president. Later that evening, Wednesday, I appeared on television addressing the situation; the government would discuss and decide on restrictions the following day. After the show I called Kiuru to go through the plan again, and she said we might need to introduce the Emergency Powers Act, a huge decision that grants more powers to the government during emergencies like war and pandemics. I agreed with her, and we started planning how to do this in a structured way without causing panic. I stayed awake well after midnight thinking about the next few days, when not just our decisions but their timing would be critical. When I woke up very early the next morning everything clicked—all the disparate pieces of information fell into place. I knew exactly how I would lead the process, and I sent a message to my advisors that everyone should come to Kesäranta, the prime minister's residence, to work on steps together as soon as possible.

Looking back, things seem more streamlined than they actually were. In the early days of the pandemic the whole administrative machinery was in shock; even very experienced public officials didn't know how to deal with the new reality. At the time epidemiologists at THL also had varying views on how to react to the threat. Should we let the virus sweep across the country and build a natural resistance to the disease, or should we try to prevent the virus from spreading and protect the lives and health of our most vulnerable citizens? I had a strong opinion that we had to do the latter and impose strict restrictions at a relatively early stage so we could keep infections as low as possible. We knew we couldn't escape infections altogether, but we could lower the curve of the spread and keep most of our citizens safe. We were also concerned about the capacity of our healthcare system and especially intensive care services, which required a lot of specialized personnel and equipment.

In times of disruption, when established structures of governance can't fully meet the task at hand, the need for strong political leadership is evident. I had a plan. We would close what amounted to the entire country within a week, and we would have to do it without even having all necessary tools and legislation. This required as much agreement as possible, so all key institutions would need to back the government's plan, and it would also require extremely clear communication with the public.

When my advisors gathered at Kesäranta Thursday morning, March 12, I explained the steps we would take.

First we met with the government to cease public events over five hundred participants, as well as restrictions for travel and for avoiding close contact in workplaces, schools, and public places. As we didn't actually have many legal powers to do this, we formulated the restrictions as recommendations, but communicated them in our press conferences in a way that made them sound stricter. We simply didn't have another choice. These press conferences became a crucial part of controlling the situation, especially in the beginning of the pandemic. They were widely watched, and I tried to communicate in a calm and decisive manner to build trust and cooperation.

I had discussed the situation with the speaker of parliament, Matti Vanhanen, several times during the week, and he gave me an extremely useful piece of advice. He had been prime minister when the disastrous earthquake and tsunami in the Indian Ocean killed hundreds of thousands of people in 2004, 179 of them Finnish citizens. He told me that the government should hold a press conference every day, even if there aren't new decisions to announce. This would prevent false information from spreading and give me more control over the narrative. I valued his advice highly. He was among those that truly helped our government to deal with the situation. His attitude was that no necessary action should be left undone because of the parliament. This was crucial as we had to push through so much new legislation at a very fast pace.

After the first announcement of the restrictions, I called a meeting with all the parliamentary groups to discuss Finland's response to COVID and the possibility of using the Emergency Powers Act for the first time since World War II. The use of such legislation required broad consensus among parliament, and I wanted to make sure everything was bulletproof before making public statements on the matter. I had two goals for the gathering: first, to let the groups elaborate on what kind of measures they were willing to enact, and second to have their approval for the use of the Emergency Powers Act. All groups were ready to use the legislation if it was necessary, and most were amenable to stricter restrictions as well. I was relieved— I knew we would have to engage those restrictions very soon.

On Friday the 13th, we held a meeting with the president and the Ministerial Committee on Foreign and Security Policy, a platform that is used to cooperate between institutions, to discuss COVID and the possibility of announcing emergency conditions, which was a requirement before the government could use the Emergency Powers Act. The president stated that in his opinion the conditions were already in place and the government could act as it deemed necessary.

A few hours later, after another session in the parliament, we convened with key ministers to organize the necessary steps. The two ministers from STM were already preparing new, stricter restrictions, and the minister of education, Li Andersson, prepared for Finland's schools to move to distance learning and planned to recommend that families keep children at home instead of taking them to daycare. All of this was a lot of work, and we didn't have much time. So we worked through the weekend and met in Kesäranta several times to draft the guidelines and a long list of restrictions that would lock down the entire country at the beginning of the next week.

On Sunday, March 15, I asked the four other party leaders of the government—Katri Kulmuni, Maria Ohisalo, Li Andersson, and Anna-Maja Henriksson—to meet me at Kesäranta to go through everything. The minister of economic affairs, Mika Lintilä, was also present as we had to discuss what the restrictions would mean for the private sector and how we would compensate for the massive business losses we predicted. We needed to decide on a supplementary budget of an unprecedented scale, and to meet with the central labor market organizations as we required their help to put remote work recommendations into practice. This was scheduled for the next evening.

For the restrictions to work, they had to be as comprehensive as possible. This meant reducing contacts in workplaces, schools and daycare, in public services and transportation, and in all kinds of events and places where people meet. We were also preparing travel restrictions and the closure of our borders. This wasn't as straightforward as we would have wanted; restrictions and their justifications were different at external than internal EU borders and the Schengen Area borders that include twenty-nine European countries without border control in normal circumstances. Closing the eastern external border with Russia was relatively easy. Coordinating with our western neighbors Norway and especially Sweden was more difficult. Our shared internal borders meant that many people commuted between our countries every day, and in some cities the border even runs through the middle.

Throughout the pandemic, Sweden had a radically different COVID policy from the rest of the Nordic countries, and this caused many kinds of practical problems beyond the border: their policy was to impose lesser restrictions. Sweden's neighboring countries—Finland, Denmark, and Norway—imposed heavy restrictions early on. This meant that Sweden's infection numbers were much higher than ours, and we worried this would cause skyrocketing infection rates in nearby regions of Finland. I remember my close colleague, the Swedish prime minister Stefan Löfven, being surprised about our decision to move to distance learning in schools.

The next day, March 16, the government decided that Finland was in a state of emergency. I called the president to make sure he still agreed to the conditions to make the declaration official. Now we could activate the Emergency Powers Act, which allowed us to concentrate power in the hands of the government and impose much stricter restrictions than before. After working nonstop the whole weekend, we had prepared a list of nineteen restrictions and recommendations. These included limiting public gatherings to ten people, closing all but critical public services and buildings, and going to remote schooling. Borders that remained a constant worry throughout the pandemic were on the list as well. Because we didn't have legislation in place for closing restaurants and private businesses, we needed a set of new laws to do this. We were building the ship while we rowed it.

Even though the public was expecting something like this, I think the nation was shocked by the severity of the situation. Because Finland is relatively geographically isolated, COVID had not yet arrived in full force like it had in some other countries. And because we acted so decisively and relatively early, we were able to keep infection rates under control. Our restrictions were also more moderate, and lasted for shorter periods, than in many other places. But the shock made citizens alert and more willing to follow the guidelines, which were still partly voluntary. At the same time it was important that the measures felt proportionate so we wouldn't see a backlash.

Topics of discussion were much the same in Finland as they were elsewhere around the world. People went to the grocery store in a panic and hoarded toilet paper, pasta, and canned food, causing shortages in some shops. Announcing that we had plenty of toilet paper in the country—we have a large, traditional pulp and paper industry—did nothing to stop this. It became clear that people were afraid and wanted to do anything to ameliorate their risk of suffering.

○

Another strange thing about the COVID era was that, while it was a very hectic time, I wasn't traveling. For several months I spent all my time in just a few places: the prime minister's office, the House of Estates—a historical government property used for negotiations and meetings—parliament, and Kesäranta, the official residence of the prime minister. Markus and I had planned to keep our main home in Tampere, but because of the pandemic, it made most sense for him and Emma to move to Helsinki. Markus, like many people at the time, was working remotely, and took care of Emma at home because daycare was closed. Realistically, I would never have been able to take even a day off to go to Tampere, and this way I was able to see them at least at some point during the day.

In the first waves of COVID, Finland ranked very low in infections and deaths, and our economy wasn't hit as harshly as those of many other European countries. Our government's so-called hybrid strategy was based on three principles: prevent the spread of the virus, secure the healthcare capacity, and protect high-risk populations. Putting people's lives and health at the center of our policy also protected our economy and made the business environment as predictable as it could be in the middle of a crisis. But forcing restrictions wasn't easy, and we were constantly trying to balance rights that were at odds with each other: the right to live and to stay healthy, the right to work and earn a living, the right of children to education and to play.

None of us in the government wanted to restrict people's lives, but we had no choice. And as spring progressed, restrictions had to be extended and new ones imposed—the most drastic was that we had to isolate the capital and surrounding regions from the rest of Finland, where infection rates were more moderate, to prevent overwhelming rural hospital capacity. Throughout the pandemic, different measures were in place in different regions, depending on the disease situation, and the restrictions were lifted as soon as they were no longer necessary in a particular area. This meant continuous negotiations within the government.

For a long time, my life consisted of the same routine: waking up very early to get ready for the day that was always packed, leading negotiations, telling people about the situation and new decisions at press conferences, going to the parliament, and then coming home late and spending the rest of the evening on the phone with our ministers or experts planning the next day's negotiations. The first weeks and months of COVID meant key ministers, officials, and experts worked endlessly. I had my first half day off on Sunday, March 22, and I went for a walk with my family. By the time I got back home I had a mountain of work waiting on my desk.

Because we didn't have much knowledge about the virus at the beginning—how easily and exponentially it spread, how long it was contagious, what symptoms it caused immediately and in the long term, and how all this would strain our healthcare capacity—we had to make decisions based on probabilities and best guesses. It took a lot of courage, as well as the ability to set emotions and fears aside. I had to stay extremely focused and absorb huge amounts of information from a field I wasn't very familiar with. Most of the time I managed to turn my personal feelings off just to be able to work effectively, but the shock and sadness hit me when I woke up each morning. Every day, however, I got out of bed and started completing the day's tasks as if on autopilot.

Even though the situation was extremely stressful, most of the time I felt in control and that I had a mission—it was like being inside the eye of a hurricane. My stress began to manifest in physical symptoms. First a twitch in my eye, later a roughness in my throat. My stomach was constantly upset and I started losing weight. The scariest symptoms came later, when in a stressful situation I lost my vision so that everything blurred for an entire day; I couldn't read any texts or recognize people's facial features. I think that even today I still carry a lot of mental burden from those years, but my mind has built barriers to protect itself.

As I mentioned, the most difficult thing to manage in the first wave of COVID was the lack of knowledge. Our government was dedicated to leading with the best and most up-to-date information, and we changed our strategy many times in response. At times we were criticized for being too reactive, but often this was the only way to manage the situation as circumstances changed and the virus mutated. I still believe our willingness to update our strategy when faced with new information was one of the reasons Finland coped so well. We acknowledged our mistakes, and didn't let our pride stop us from doing what was necessary.

Even though there were many other difficulties—lack of legislation and medical equipment, problems at airports and border regions, rising infections in care homes and hospitals, complications in developing compensation models for the private sector—we came through, not perfectly, but good enough. Students could continue going to lessons through distance-learning platforms, and teachers were incredibly flexible and competent in handling their new, unprecedented responsibilities. Our healthcare system didn't crumble, and doctors and nurses put their own lives at risk to care for people. People in the service sector made sure that our basic needs were covered, and our industries didn't stop manufacturing while putting safety protocols in place. People showed resilience and trusted that the pressure would ease.

○

As the weather got warmer, the stress of the pandemic finally began to abate. At the end of April 2020, we started discussing how and when to lift some of the restrictions. In some ways, negotiating how to reopen society was as difficult as closing things down. The first phase of the crisis was defined by urgency; decisions were made based on necessity, and the debates we had around them were relatively streamlined because we had no time to waste. Reopening had to be managed more delicately. While of course everyone was eager to resume their lives, we knew we couldn't simply lift all the restrictions at once. We had to open gradually and expand our testing capacity to make sure our decisions didn't unleash a new wave of infections.

Restrictions were first lifted from schools and children's activities, and gradually the rest of society, except for mass events, followed. People were relieved and hopeful that the worst was over and life was returning to a state that was as normal as possible. And I had another, more personal reason to be happy. Markus and I had been together for sixteen years and engaged since the summer of 2016. We had planned to have a wedding for many years, but some obstacle had always stopped us from going through with it: a venue going under renovation, being pregnant with Emma, or both of us just working too much. But that summer we decided that even if the timing wasn't perfect—and there were still restrictions and recommendations for gatherings over fifty people—we would get married on August 1. (Actually, we set two different days for the wedding just in case some sudden work situation needed my attention, and we confirmed the official date to our guests only a few days before.) Neither of us belonged to a church, so we held the ceremony at Kesäranta, in front of an old pier by the sea. Afterward, we had a small, beautiful celebration in the courtyard under the trees, which were decorated with paper lanterns, listening to jazz and bossa nova. We had forty guests, just relatives and some close friends, and we were lucky it was sunny all day. We were able to keep the wedding a secret and only announced afterward that we had gotten married.

Another happy, though surreal, moment for me took place at the end of the summer, when the SDP held a party conference in my home city Tampere, to elect me as its party leader. The situation was unique: usually, a politician would become a party leader before she becomes the prime minister, and it would be a major stepping-stone in her career, because party leaders are very powerful in Finnish politics. But because of all the tumult of the elections, we had done it the other way around. COVID meant we had to impose different kinds of safety measures for the gathering, but the pandemic affected the event otherwise as well; people were exceptionally united—usually there would be lively debate and criticism—and showed me strong support. Years earlier, as a young participant in the party congress, I had been among those who were critical of our policies, but the absence of political conflicts that weekend was welcome. When reporters asked me what I'd done before I showed up to the party conference, I told them truthfully that I'd used the opportunity to return to Tampere to clean our home there. It had been sitting empty for months.

○

The increased sunlight and warm weather helped us lower infections dramatically, and the government's strategy for lifting restrictions was successful as well—I remember one day in July when only one or two new COVID cases were reported to the government. But as fall approached, the numbers started to rise again. We knew we were heading into a new wave of the disease, which experts had predicted at the beginning of the pandemic. The virus would appear in different mutations periodically, and we would have to adapt our society to this new normal.

In August, the Finnish Institute for Health and Welfare (THL) recommended that the entire population, except for children and those whose medical conditions didn't allow it, wear masks. This may sound late to people in other countries. Before this, THL hadn't been willing to recommend wearing masks because there wasn't scientific proof that wearing them at a population level would actually help. Inside the institute, as well as in the health ministry, there were conflicting views. For me, it was important that these kinds of recommendations for using medical equipment were made by health authorities and not by politicians. Still, the matter had already been politicized in the spring; some groups had demanded that we make masks obligatory, which we never did, not only because authorities didn't recommend it but also because, like many countries, we didn't have enough supply in our stores for the entire population to use them correctly. We had reserves of basic food and medical equipment in case of national emergencies, but we didn't have enough masks to cover the entire population every single day. Like most other countries, we rationed our initial supplies for healthcare workers and hospitals, and sought to prioritize groups most in need, and even then there were shortages.

Of course, the government was blamed for not having enough masks in our emergency supply warehouses—Finland is known to be a country of preparedness. We had more than many other countries, but we needed so much more than anyone could have expected. Like everyone else, we spent the entire spring trying to purchase masks, but the process was complicated and caused many problems. The minister in charge of the purchase, Aino-Kaisa Pekonen, explained over and over again that we had done what we could to prepare, but she was heavily criticized by the opposition and press. Later, she said a weight was lifted from her shoulders when her party, the Left Alliance, had a preplanned ministerial reshuffle in 2021 and she was relieved of her duties.

The shortage of masks became a convenient political weapon for the opposition to criticize the government with, but it wasn't anywhere near the most frustrating problem of the COVID crisis for me as prime minister. Constantly handling multiple problems from big ones to tiny details was exhausting. We had several situations where individuals and organizations were reluctant to take responsibility for certain issues if they weren't strictly defined as their task alone. One of the most well-known cases was the handling of safety protocols at our largest airport, Helsinki-Vantaa: making sure people with symptoms were tested and that passengers followed all the instructions in place. The protocols themselves weren't the root problem, but the question of who was in charge of the airport's safety regulations. It turned out to be impossible to get things done without specific guidance from the government, meaning we had to micromanage safety operations at the airport so that various groups didn't get into disagreements about who was responsible for what. It felt like professionals had suddenly transformed into children who had to be held by the hand to do their jobs. At one point I became so irritated by the ordeal that I said maybe we should send ministers to the airport to put up tape and signs to get things done.

Nevertheless, despite the difficulties, I would say that in a crisis, Finland showed its strength: the collective good was prioritized, and people and organizations were proud to help each other through this scary, uncertain time. Healthcare professionals did unbelievable work in unprecedented circumstances—we couldn't have survived without their dedication and strength. But as the pandemic dragged on, people got more and more tired. When autumn 2020 arrived and we had to impose restrictions again, we faced a new problem in managing the situation. At the beginning of COVID everyone followed the government's instructions because people were scared, frozen in response to the new situation. But as everyone got used to the threat, people started to express more opinions on how society should respond to it, and different players with power, like municipalities, started pulling in different directions. It became much more difficult to lead in a centralized way. Some officials preferred certain restrictions over others, and a few didn't want any restrictions whatsoever. Kiuru, who by then had become known as "the minister for COVID," kept pushing the regional governments to control their own outbreaks, and I continued to lead the endless negotiations concerning restrictions. Because decisions varied in different regions, people got confused about what was going on and where. We simply couldn't communicate in a way that was as streamlined as before.

As we tried our best to control the new wave of infections and the challenging environment we had to operate in, we were also looking hopefully forward to the vaccines under development to help us. Without the common purchase and distribution of vaccines within the EU, small countries like Finland would have had a much harder time providing vaccinations to our population at such an early stage. I would say this was one of the biggest successes of the EU during COVID. The first vaccines in Finland were provided to healthcare workers in December 2020; after this, we were able to gradually vaccinate our adult population. I got my first vaccine on June 11, 2021. There was something very Finnish about not letting even the prime minister jump the queue; we vaccinated all people on the basis of their age and condition. I am very proud of this feature of our society: an expectation that our rules are fair and just, and will be followed by everyone equally, is one of the reasons there is such a deep sense of trust among our people.

○

We had managed to control the epidemic during autumn 2020 using only the regular powers of authorities, and with the help of new legislation that we'd created since the beginning of the pandemic, and we had already dismantled the emergency conditions in June that year. But in February 2021, a more contagious virus variant emerged. The state of emergency came into effect again on March 1, and the Emergency Powers Act was reintroduced. We had evaluated the situation during fall and early spring and updated the government's hybrid strategy several times. We had also prepared even heavier restrictions if the situation wasn't controlled otherwise.

The most controversial of these was a general restriction of movement within cities with the highest infection numbers. Many countries in Europe had introduced different versions of this, for example restrictions based on the time or location when and where people could go out. So it wasn't unprecedented or even rare, but in Finland it was met with a lot of resistance. The experts from THL were telling the government that it was necessary to introduce these measures to make sure our hospital capacity would be able to weather the new variant, but the proposal was hard to get through initial phases, and then the parliament's Constitutional Committee stopped the legislation from passing. The committee determined it was not as necessary and proportionate to restrict people's basic rights this way. We had introduced all the restrictions that were possible with the powers we had, and we had to pray they would be enough to keep the situation under control. Luckily, soon after, the numbers started to gradually decline.

The knockout of this legislation was embarrassing to the government, but out of all the restrictions that we had to impose, the restrictions concerning children and young people were the most difficult—we knew that they would have a long-term impact on their education and well-being. The restrictions also affected various sectors differently, and the culture industry was among the ones that was hit unfairly hard because of event and gathering closures. So during the summer and fall 2021, when infections eased and we were granted a much needed moment of freedom, I met with representatives from the arts to show them the government was thinking of them and to attempt to find ways to rebuild trust.

One evening I invited people from the music industry to Kesäranta to talk about the challenges they'd faced. The meeting went well, and I was pleased with the discussion, but the next day things quickly spiraled into a crisis. The repercussions of the pandemic weren't the only problem the culture sector was facing. In Finland, the state controls a large portion of gambling revenue through a public monopoly and uses the funds for various ventures, including culture, science, sports, youth organizations, and social and healthcare NGOs. But the flow of income had been declining, which caused a problem for everyone who received these funds. We had agreed that we would negotiate a solution, because the situation was becoming critical given the COVID restrictions on top of everything else.

Two days later, the minister of science and culture, a member of

the Center Party, who had of course attended the meeting in Kesäranta, held a press conference announcing cuts for the culture sector.
He hadn't told me he was going to go public with the issue, and he
knew this funding was still being negotiated; it was a political maneu-
ver to pressurize the issue in their favor. If the point of the meeting
the night before had been to rebuild trust with culture workers, this
announcement seemed like a huge betrayal. I was furious. I invited
the leaders of the government to my office. I was in a particularly bad
mood when they arrived, and I told everyone that we weren't leaving
the office until we reversed these proposed cuts, which we did after
a few quarrelsome hours.

My reason for getting so frustrated was that if we lost the trust of
people and different groups, the consequences could be irreversible
and disastrous. We needed to recognize people's pain and distress.
We needed to reassure everyone that the government's actions and
decisions were necessary, and that we were doing everything in our
power to ease the situation. If you lose that trust once, it's incredibly
hard to build back.

○

In 2021, while all this was going on, I began to pay more attention
to my own health and started exercising regularly. After spending so
much time sitting at my desk, I'd hurt my back very badly. A couple
of times, the pain was so severe that I couldn't stand, which, even
during a pandemic, wasn't a practical way for the prime minister to
govern. So I started to walk distances during the workday instead of

taking the car. Later, after I had built up my strength, I began to run in the morning or after work. Even though it took time out of my workday, it made me more productive and became a way to relieve stress. As I was jogging, I argued with myself inside my head about everything that was bothering me. If we'd had bad negotiations one day, or if a minister had done something that annoyed me, I tried to deal with my emotions so they wouldn't influence my work. I also got a lot of energy from sports. Because Kesäranta has a basketball court, I started shooting hoops. Some of the security staff used to play basketball when they were young, so sometimes they'd join in to play basketball with me.

I began shooting hoops in the spring of 2021, and decided that I wanted to be able to hit ten free throws in a row by midsummer. While I didn't have a lot of time to practice, I used every moment I had. On many occasions, Emma was playing somewhere on the court or nearby in the big yard. I've always been able to sleep well, even in the middle of most distressing situations, but because I was working so much I simply didn't have enough time for a full night's sleep. So I got the energy that I crucially needed from sports and these breaks.

Still, it wasn't easy to make ten free throws in a row. I'd hit seven or eight shots before missing one. By the time midsummer came around, I was anxious: I knew I could do it, but I wasn't quite getting there. I had just flown back from the European Council meeting, and spent a couple of hours on the court trying to meet my goal. When I did, I was ecstatic. Not to be outdone, Markus—a much better player than I am by all accounts—went outside the next day and shot ten free throws in a row, too.

○

We were able to keep restrictions moderate in autumn 2021: enough of the population was vaccinated, and we introduced a COVID pass based on the EU's digital certificate for people that had been vaccinated, received a negative test result, or recovered from COVID. Restaurants and services were open, people could go to events, and generally live their lives. When a new variant, Omicron, forced us to reintroduce restrictions again around the holidays, as infections skyrocketed and hospitals received more and more patients, we were naturally worried that the need for intensive care would rise rapidly, but this didn't happen. That gave us hope we wouldn't have to reintroduce the most difficult restrictions. And for the first time since the beginning of the pandemic, I found myself disagreeing with our COVID minister, Kiuru, who was still in favor of heavier restrictions. The balance between different needs and rights had changed, and there were no longer sufficient grounds for all the measures. The restrictions had begun to do more harm than good.

Until this point I had been a central figure handling Finland's COVID response and leading negotiations. But when Christmas arrived, I had to step down from this role and remove myself—as well as the minister for foreign affairs and minister of defense—from the COVID-19 working group, and turn my attention toward a new threat emerging from the east. I had a bad feeling that we were heading toward even more turbulent times, as Russia started amassing troops near Ukraine's borders.

# 7.

# WAKING UP TO WAR

When the 2019 parliamentary elections were held in Finland, my political party the Social Democrats were, like most of the parliamentary parties and the vast majority of citizens, against pursuing membership in NATO, the North Atlantic Treaty Organization that has functioned as a collective security alliance for its members since it was established in 1949. In Finland, politicians running for office fill out surveys or "election compasses" on various issues, which are then publicized to communicate their stances; in the surveys I took in 2019, I answered that Finland should remain militarily nonaligned, which had been our position for decades.

But as I gained more direct experience in international debates on foreign and security policy, my views on military nonalignment and NATO started to change. We had many discussions in the European Council about how the EU could be more effective in protecting the continent from outside threats, from hybrid to cybersecurity threats to the tightening geopolitical reality. We had several strategic discussions on Russia and China and how the EU should position itself in relation to these countries. Over the decades, the EU has developed a common foreign and security policy, and it coordinates today many aspects of defense policy as well, but the EU has no mandate on defense itself; that responsibility belongs to individual member states. However, most member states have organized their national defense as part of NATO. While defense was addressed in the EU in contexts of general security and preparedness, it soon became clear to me that not being a NATO member meant being excluded from many conversations that directly affected Finland.

Before Russia started its full-scale invasion in Ukraine in 2022, Finland and Sweden—another historically militarily neutral country—were in favor of strengthening the EU's defense capabilities, as were many other member states. But at the time, there were twenty-one EU countries also in NATO, so even if the overall will was to enhance common defense capabilities, the NATO states worried that doing so would only create an extra and unnecessary layer of decision-making and security infrastructure when NATO already served this purpose. As a result, the countries that were not part of NATO were left out of critical decision-making on defense. It made less and less sense for Finland and Sweden to be excluded from these discussions.

About a year after I took office, in January 2021, I was in an online

European Council meeting when discussion turned to the worrying situation in Russia. The month before, an investigative team had determined that the country had been responsible for the poisoning of the opposition leader Alexei Navalny the previous August, and Navalny had just been arrested and sentenced to prison a few days before the meeting. Russia was becoming increasingly hostile, and the EU was beginning to see real effects of the country's authoritarian turn. Just six months earlier, we had witnessed a devastating presidential election in Belarus that Organization for Security and Cooperation in Europe (OSCE) election observers condemned as neither free nor fair, leading to the re-election of Alexander Lukashenko by, allegedly, more than 80 percent of the vote. The mass protests that followed were suppressed violently, and many peaceful protestors and citizens were arbitrarily thrown in jail. The events made clear the country had descended to dictatorship, and all of it was done with backing from Russia.

In parallel with the European Council meeting, there was an ongoing discussion in Finland regarding the use of our territory in conflict situations. The discussion started with a sentence in a government report on Finnish foreign and security policy that stated: "Finland does not allow its territory to be used for hostile purposes." The wording led to a debate between those who defended that as a clear position of avoiding Finland becoming a party in a military conflict, and those who feared that it would send a wrong signal of the country's commitment as a member of the EU. The official interpretation was that the sentence did not restrict the use of territory in conflict situations. We would need to be able to ask for all kinds of military help in case we were attacked, even if some other country would consider that as "hostile." And, if another EU member state would need help,

Finland would not be an outsider when security in our neighborhood or elsewhere in Europe was threatened.

As soon as the European Council meeting was over, I talked to my close advisors who had followed the discussion. I was troubled by the situation in Russia and the growing hostilities toward opposition and civil rights there, and by the implications of Finland's unique geopolitical position. I turned to my EU sherpa, a type of senior diplomat assigned to a prime minister for EU affairs, Jari Luoto.

"Jari, aren't you a NATO man?" I asked. I knew he had been a supporter of Finland joining NATO ever since he was an EU advisor for the government in the 1990s—a relatively rare position for anyone in Finland to have held.

He smiled and replied with a nod. This was the first time I said out loud that my view on NATO had changed. We talked about the situation and, in particular, discussed how we might begin changing our position on NATO within the SDP—we would first have to transition from negative to neutral, and then later we could come out in support of NATO membership.

My advisors and I agreed we should start, gently, to initiate some conversations about NATO before the SDP party congress that would take place in 2023. The overall time frame for NATO accession was "eventually." I thought it might take five to ten years.

○

A few things are useful to know in order to understand the Finnish mindset concerning Russia, NATO, and the foundation of our foreign and security policy. Before our independence in 1917, Finland was occupied in turns by neighboring powers from both the west and the east. We were ruled for a long, but disjointed, time by the Swedish Kingdom—from the fourteenth century to the beginning of the nineteenth century. Swedish rule ended in 1809, during the Finnish War, when Finland was occupied by Imperial Russia. After the war, Emperor Alexander I granted the country autonomy within the empire, but Swedish remained the only official language until 1863. Ever since then, Finland has had two official languages: Finnish and Swedish.

It is not wrong to say that Finland had special relations with Russia. We were more autonomous than other regions ruled by the Russian Empire. Finnish language, culture, and national identity were actually strengthened during Russian rule. Our capital was moved from Turku, on the west coast, to Helsinki, which is closer to Russia and its capital at the time, Saint Petersburg. Our administration and legislation continued to evolve under Russian rule. The rise of nationalism in Finland, combined with the collapse of the Russian Empire during World War I, led to our declaration of independence on December 6, 1917. The country was quickly recognized by the new Bolshevik government in what became the Soviet Union.

But this was a turbulent time in Finland. Quickly after the declaration of independence, the country slid into a brutal civil war that grew out of the deep discontent of the working classes and divergent views on how the new Finnish society and state should be organized. The war ended in the defeat of the socialist Red Guards in May 1918. The war has been given a variety of names, depending on the political leaning of the historical interpretation: some call it simply the Finnish

Civil War, but others refer to it as the Finnish Class War, the Finnish Revolution, or the Red Rebellion.

For decades afterward, the Finnish civil war was an open wound for the Finns. The nation only came together again during the notorious Finnish Winter War, which began in the middle of World War II in 1939. Then, Finns from different classes united as brothers in arms in the face of a common enemy, the Soviet Union.

Even though Finland was able to resist the Soviet Union's incursions into its territory for longer than expected, we had to concede after three-and-a-half months, in March 1940, and sign a treaty that granted about one-tenth of our territory to the Soviet Union. Fighting nevertheless continued in the country, and the Continuation War was fought from 1941 to 1944. Ultimately, we were able to preserve our independence, but it came with a heavy cost of lives, territory, and substantial reparations. Almost half a million Finnish citizens who lived in ceded regions like Karelia had to be evacuated and resettled throughout Finland. Still, we consider ourselves fortunate compared to the countries—including our neighbor, Estonia—that were occupied and forced to live under the Soviet regime. We were able to rebuild and develop our country as an independent democracy—if not fully part of the West, not behind the Iron Curtain either.

In the decades that followed, Finland had to balance our desire to deepen our connection to the West with the reality of the threats presented by our aggressive, and much larger, neighbor. There was a strong tension between accommodating the wishes of the Soviet Union and the forces of integration with the West. Finland became a member of the UN in 1955 after resistance from the Soviet Union, and we also managed a free trade agreement with the European Economic Community in 1973. The Conference on Security and Cooperation in Europe was held in Helsinki in 1975, where the Helsinki Accords were signed. In hindsight this could be seen as a major event in Finland's Westernization. But the reality was that the Soviet Union significantly limited our movements on the world stage, and these limits also poisoned our internal culture and politics. For decades, Finnish media and culture often self-censored, refraining from criticizing the USSR, and books and films considered "anti-Soviet" were rare.

In international relations, the situation gave rise to its own term: *Finlandization*. We were an independent and sovereign nation, but in practice we had to restrain ourselves out of fear of provoking the USSR—especially when it came to foreign and security policy. We also maintained strong links to the East because of war reparations and trade. Finnish presidents and other key politicians had to maintain strong personal connections to the USSR, and our media became increasingly biased as well. Finlandization has been offered from time to time as a solution for conflicts and maintaining peace in similar circumstances. It's not a road that I would recommend or wish for any country.

The relationship Finland has had with Russia has been more pragmatic than warm or good. We share the longest border with Russia of all EU and NATO countries, over thirteen hundred kilometers. This geographical fact can't be put aside. It is important to understand that even though we have a long history with Russia, Finland and Finnish people have always identified themselves as being part of the Nordic culture and region. We do not have the cultural or linguistic connections to Russia or a Slavic heritage that some neighboring countries have.

This is the context in which Finland refrained from joining NATO, a security apparatus that was established to protect its members from Soviet threats at the beginning of the Cold War. After the Soviet Union collapsed in 1991, we were finally able to take significant steps toward integrating with the West. This meant applying to be a member state of the European Union in March 1992, and Finns voted to join the bloc in October 1994. For many of those who voted in favor, it was about security. Ever since, the EU has been the foundation of our security architecture. But we still carried the collective memory of our difficult history with Russia and the political burdens of Finlandization, so we maintained a doctrine of stability through cooperation with Russia. Pragmatic, concrete cooperation and dialogue were also means of monitoring what Russia was up to. Although Russia did not pose an acute military threat to Finland anymore, we couldn't forget everything we'd suffered over the twentieth century. Maintaining both our independence and our security was very important to Finnish people, and for a long time that meant staying out of NATO—which Russia considers to be threatening—and maintaining a functional relationship with Russia.

After the Cold War ended, the general feeling in the West was that the great ideological battle of our time was won, and our democratic values had prevailed. Russia even began to take steps toward democracy and Western values. International cooperation, globalization, and cooperation on global trade became accepted norms. As a result, many countries in Europe reduced defense spending. A new sense of security reigned. The money, they believed, was better spent elsewhere.

Finland's history meant we chose another path. While most of the Western world was overtaken by a general optimism, we remained prepared for the worst. Finland maintained mandatory military service and made significant investments in defense. One example of this is the purchasing of F/A-18 Hornets in 1992, which at the time caused a big debate, in part because the fighter jets came from the USA. (The decision was prepared under the leadership of Finland's first female defense minister, Elisabeth Rehn.) Even today, Finland maintains one of the most substantial wartime armies in Europe, not only relative to the size of the population but in absolute terms: our wartime strength is almost 280,000 soldiers, and total reserves reach almost 900,000. In surveys in which people are asked about their willingness to defend their country, Finland ranks first in the West. Strong and credible national defense has always been the cornerstone of our security. One aspect of our collective memory is that we have been left too alone in war; too alone in securing peace. We've always had to fend for ourselves.

Still, it wasn't as if we were isolated. Since the end of the Cold War, Finland has strengthened its ties with Western partners—the Nordic countries and especially Sweden, the United States, the United Kingdom, and NATO. By the time I took office, NATO was no longer a bad word, but most voters and political parties were against joining the alliance. In a 2019 survey conducted by *Helsingin Sanomat*, the largest subscription newspaper in the country, only 20 percent of respondents were in favor of applying to NATO; 56 percent were against and 24 percent did not know. In March 2022, just after the war in Ukraine began, 48 percent were in favor and only 27 percent were against. The change was dramatic, and the reason was Russia.

After the Finnish constitution was reformed in 2000, the power to make foreign and security policy decisions was distributed among the president, the government, and parliament. The president leads foreign policy in cooperation with the government. The government proposes courses of action, prepares and executes foreign policy, and ultimately is responsible to the parliament. Without cooperation and the assent of the government, there is no action. The constitution dictates very clear guidelines for which entities have the right to receive what kinds of information, or approve agreements, but in general the glue that holds together our foreign and security policy is a will to consensus. Consensus is at the core of our foreign and security policy for a reason: Russia. We are a small country next to a big, aggressive neighbor, and we do not have the luxury of disagreeing on the nation's security; any public disagreement might suggest weakness and make us seem vulnerable to attack.

Finland's updated official view on NATO was defined in a government report on foreign and security policy, drafted in collaboration with the president and parliament and approved in fall 2020. It reads:

> *Maintaining national room to maneuver and freedom of choice are also integral parts of Finland's foreign, security and defense policy. This retains the option of joining a military alliance and applying for NATO membership. Decisions are always considered in real time, taking account of the changes in the international security environment. Interoperability achieved through cooperation ensures the elimination of any practical impediments arising to a potential membership.*

In other words, Finland could have applied for NATO membership at the time: the emphasis on flexibility in response to changing conditions was new. We didn't have a consensus to apply to NATO then, but in 2022, when we changed our national position on military nonalignment, this part of the report gave us a valuable basis for the discussion. Up until 2022, it was a widely shared view that Finland would be safer remaining outside of military alliances because our positioning had been successful so far.

And then it was no longer a successful strategy. It wasn't safe not to join.

○

From the outside, it might have felt as if everything changed overnight, but in reality the relationship between Russia and the EU had been deteriorating for months leading up to the full-scale war in Ukraine. In addition to the military aggression, Russia had also attacked the entire continent by weaponizing its energy deliveries to the European market. Long before the invasion, Russia had begun to reduce gas deliveries to ensure European gas storages wouldn't be full the next winter. After the attack in February 2022, they cut the gas supply massively, resulting in extremely high energy prices, inflation, and threats to many industries.

Many European countries had relied in good faith on Russia for critical resources. The conventional wisdom in Europe was that close economic ties with Russia would prevent wider war and further hostilities—this was the basis of Finland's policy of not rocking the boat. And even if relations between the EU and Russia had deteriorated since 2014 as a consequence of Russia's illegal annexation of Crimea and the war in eastern Ukraine, many countries, like

Germany, continued to rely on Russia. The highly controversial Nord Stream 2 pipeline was supposed to link Russia to Germany through the Baltic Sea and begin delivering gas in the fall of 2021. Eventually it couldn't open because the US placed sanctions on companies contributing to the project. The justification for the sanctions was that the pipeline would increase European dependence on Russian energy, which the US considered, correctly, a vulnerability. At the time, more than 40 percent of the natural gas in Europe was supplied by Russia. It's important to understand that when Putin began using the EU's economic dependence on Russia as a weapon, it was a political move: a way of using our own beliefs and failed logic to weaken public support for Ukraine through high energy prices and inflation.

At the same time gas prices were rising, Russia amplified its rhetoric around the territorial disputes in Ukraine. As the West tried to find diplomatic solutions, Putin continued to aggravate the already tense situation. In December 2021 Putin demanded that NATO rule out further expansion to the east. This was not well received in Finland, which is of course to the east of NATO. Many leaders in the West thought Putin's aim was to build up pressure so that Russia would have a better negotiating stance on Ukraine. On January 26, 2022, Germany, France, Ukraine, and Russia held a Normandy Format meeting in Paris, a type of forum first convened in 2014 after the invasion of Crimea, to try to de-escalate the situation between Russia and Ukraine. Although the group had continued to meet periodically, the agreements and mechanisms it set up for peace in the region had failed to stop the fighting; Ukraine felt pressured into accepting unfair compromises, and Russia had repeatedly violated the terms of these agreements.

In the Paris meeting all participants stated their commitment to the Minsk Agreements and their support for the continuation of the ceasefire in east Ukraine.

I was never in touch with Putin personally, because his counterpart in Finland is the president. But I did of course participate in discussions on Russia as part of our national decision making and leading our EU policy. I especially remember my trip to Berlin in October 2021 to meet with Angela Merkel just after Germany's national elections in late September 2021. The timing of the meeting made it a farewell discussion with Merkel. After serving as Germany's chancellor for sixteen years, she was finally stepping down; Olaf Scholz, then the finance minister, would take office a couple of months later. Topics ranged from European affairs to COVID to competitiveness to the EU's strategic autonomy and relations with Turkey, China, and Russia.

I had worked with Merkel a fair bit, mostly in meetings of the European Council. She was widely respected and deserved her reputation for being straightforward, tough but fair, and a good negotiator. She would often take a leading role at European Council meetings when decisions were stalled, and she was able to negotiate compromises not only from Germany's perspective but from a European perspective as well. Still, I expected her to be more at ease during our meeting. You would think that when someone has finally concluded a successful thirty-year career in politics, she would feel some relief. But the atmosphere when I walked into her office was heavy. She seemed very worried. More than anything else, I remember she seemed profoundly disappointed with Putin and with Russia in general.

Her attitude, and message, was alarming. Although she didn't say anything directly, she seemed to have some kind of intuition that things were about to get worse. The international community's desperation to find a diplomatic solution intensified. But by the middle of February 2022, Russia had sent troops to its own close regions and Belarus, on the border with Ukraine, claiming it was a drill.

○

I can vividly remember the morning when Europe woke up in war. In the weeks that preceded the invasion, we got intel from the US and the UK that Russia was planning to attack Ukraine imminently. A few EU leaders and I had demanded that the European Council convene a meeting early that week, but the European Council president, Charles Michel, did not send an invitation until late Wednesday night. Everybody hoped that Russia would back down—that the threats were just more attempts at leverage. But going to bed the night before the invasion, the atmosphere was different. The sense that everything was about to change darkened the room. My security was instructed to wake me up immediately if the invasion began.

It must have been before six in the morning when my security told me Russia had launched missile strikes across Ukraine. From then on, many things happened in a very short period of time. The president and I made statements early that morning condemning the attack. We convened with the president and the Ministerial Committee on Foreign and Security Policy to go through what was happening. I told them I would fly to Brussels later that day for an extraordinary meeting of the European Council. Along with the US, UK, and Switzerland, the European Commission had been preparing a sanction package against Russia and Belarus for months; Finland was actively participating in the secret discussions as we wanted to make sure the sanctions would be unequivocal and hit Russia hard from the beginning. Before the press conference that followed my meeting with the president and government ministers, the atmosphere in the Presidential Palace was somber. We were lost in our own thoughts, and not many words were exchanged.

The mood at the European Council was resolute. Unlike in 2014, when Russia invaded Crimea and the EU was caught by surprise, this time we were able to decide on sanctions to be put in place right away. President Zelensky participated in the meeting from Kyiv and described the horrendous situation in Ukraine. Many leaders were in tears; the empathy toward the Ukrainian people was palpable in the room. Nobody knew what would happen in the days and weeks to come. We were worried about the overall situation as well as the safety of President Zelensky, our colleague and friend.

○

For Finland, Russia's aggression toward Ukraine meant conducting a deep, but swift, assessment of our own national security. Waking up that horrific Thursday morning, I knew what was ahead for Finland. The age of military nonalignment was over, and we had to decide our position on NATO in the middle of a war. It wouldn't be easy, and it would require determination, unity, and a process that was inclusive and imperceptible at the same time. I could sense that the national mindset had changed overnight.

The president, government ministers, parliament, political parties, and key officials on foreign and security policy all played roles in the process, which had many moving parts. One major issue was that Finland needed to synchronize its NATO process with that of Sweden, and we knew the window of opportunity to get the ball rolling was very slim. There were several reasons for this: first, elections were coming up in Sweden; second, we didn't know how the situation at the Ukrainian front would evolve; and finally, we couldn't be certain about Russia's priorities after the war ended, or other great powers' willingness and ability to fight them if necessary.

Sweden's history was different from ours; their policy of military neutrality was rooted more in principles than in pragmatism. Still, it was crucial that both of our countries work toward the same outcome, at the same time. We shared the same security environment, and given that the other Nordic countries—Norway, Denmark, and Iceland—were already members of NATO, it would have posed a serious security risk for a single country to remain outside the alliance. Both sides understood this, even if it took a little bit more time for Sweden to comprehend the urgency.

The process looked efficient and coherent from outside, and I'm proud of that. But the reality was more complex, as it always is. The most devastating moment for me personally happened in the early stages of the talks. The president has a key role in foreign and security policy, and he was extremely popular with voters and had a unique relationship with the press, too. Nothing would happen without the president's involvement. But when I reached out to President Niinistö and described to him what I thought we could expect, his reaction surprised me. He replied to me that the NATO discussion was a task for parliament.

This was one of the few times during my years as a prime minister when I was truly stunned. The distribution of Finland's foreign and security policy mandate is complex, but it was not the case that the NATO discussion was up to parliament. The president was in charge in cooperation with the government. I couldn't hide my disappointment from the four other leaders of the government when I described the situation to them at the House of Estates on February 28. I knew how difficult it would be to lead the process without the full commitment of all parties and institutions, when the atmosphere throughout Europe was already extremely anxious and volatile.

The views in the government varied. The only party that had an existing positive stand on NATO was the Swedish People's Party. Historically, the other parties in government—the Social Democrats, the Center Party, the Greens, and the Left Alliance—had more or less supported military nonalignment. (The Left Alliance was the most aggressively opposed to joining NATO.) Among the opposition, which consisted of right-wing and conservative parties, the only party in favor of NATO membership was the National Coalition Party. The other three—the Finns Party, the Christian Democrats, and the Movement Now that had only one MP—leaned toward neutrality.

The discussion with the four other party leaders in government wasn't easy, but I felt their sympathy for my responsibility. Li Andersson, the leader of the Left Alliance, was not receptive to even having a discussion on NATO. In my view, Annika Saarikko, of the Center Party, had already accepted the reality of the situation and the change that was ahead; we were on the same page. Anna-Maja Henriksson, of the Swedish People's Party, was very supportive and recognized the sensitivities involved in the issue. I also sensed the Greens and their leader Maria Ohisalo would back me. Because the situation was so fragile in Europe there was one question above others: how to initiate the NATO process in Finland without being vocal about it.

I turned to the person who had been so helpful to me over these difficult years, the speaker of parliament Matti Vanhanen, and asked him what he thought about the president's reply and the parliament's role. He understood the complexity of the situation right away and mentioned the citizens' initiatives on NATO that would be submitted to parliament for consideration within a week. Even if the initiatives were not substantial enough to serve as a mandate, or in any way the go-ahead to proceed, they would create an excuse to start discussions with parliamentary groups. We convened the following day, March 1, at the parliament auditorium. I had originally invited the parliamentary groups there to discuss the national Emergency Powers Act, but eventually we discussed the dramatic security situation.

Li Andersson, of the Left Alliance, did not take the change of topic well. She was very loyal to her party's and parliamentary group's position on NATO. I remember her calling me the day before, very angry, and shouting at me that their parliamentary group wouldn't participate in any "NATO talks." I tried to calm her down and explained that it would be better for them to participate than to opt out of the meeting, so they could at least get some of their concerns heard. The following day they showed up.

Before the heated phone call from Andersson, we had just announced Finland's first arms assistance to Ukraine, which contained 2,500 assault rifles, 150,000 cartridges for attack rifles, 1,500 single-shot anti-tank weapons, and 70,000 combat ration packages. All leaders of the governing parties had agreed on the material aid package over the weekend. In the press conference that followed the decision, I was asked about the turnaround in public opinion regarding NATO. I answered:

> *"Many who have previously been against membership or were undecided have changed their stance to a positive one—and I would guess that two questions particularly influence this. Firstly, what is the border that Russia has crossed [read: Ukraine], and what is the border that it wouldn't cross [read: NATO]? The second question, of course, relates to whether we would be alone or together with others if Russia crosses a certain [read: our] border."*

Before the parliamentary groups meeting on March 1, I met with Antti Lindtman, leader of our group, and Petteri Orpo, leader of the conservative National Coalition Party, to discuss the process in parliament and to create a common understanding of the situation. I needed the support of the two biggest parliamentary groups, and from both the government and opposition, to build consensus not only on the outcome, but the path for how to get there. We could not afford to show any internal discord.

Once the meeting finally got going, it focused almost entirely on how we could support Ukraine and on the changed security situation in Europe and how to organize the process of evaluating the change within Finland's institutions. The tone of the discussion was set by the first speaker, the permanent secretary of the Ministry of Defense. He described how Russia had already failed in its original objective of quickly capturing Kyiv, said that the Ukrainians' will to fight was strong, and added that President Zelensky has already won the information war over Russia. He also mentioned that Finland's first shipment of weapons to Ukraine was on its way and that the Ministry of Defense was already mapping out material preparedness and future help Finland could provide. After a few hours of debate, I summarized the general understanding in the room: first, we had to analyze the changed security situation and all the options, and second, how the process concerning this should be organized. It may sound long-winded, but the question that needed to be addressed was simple: Should we remain militarily nonaligned, or not?

During those early days I was actively in touch with the Swedish prime minister, Magdalena Andersson, and our teams liaised regularly. After the parliamentary meeting, my sherpa, Jari Luoto, contacted key people in Andersson's cabinet and met the Swedish ambassador, Nicola Clase, at her embassy. Afterward, we heard that Clase had sent a telegram to Stockholm saying that her sense was that Finland was moving toward applying for membership in NATO.

We received an invitation from President Niinistö to discuss the situation the next day. On March 2, the president met with me and several representatives from parliament. The following day the president flew to Washington for a meeting with President Biden on Friday. Biden reaffirmed the importance of NATO's "open doors" policy to the United States. The two presidents also called the Swedish prime minister.

A Swedish delegation arrived in Helsinki on Saturday, March 5. The day started with a meeting between me and Prime Minister Andersson at Kesäranta. As fellow Social Democrats, she and I had a warm and straightforward relationship, and our meeting, with only our closest advisors present, was frank and honest. I told her that the discussion concerning NATO had started, and I predicted that it wouldn't take long for Finland to make a decision based on the atmosphere among the people and within each political party. My frankness and the time frame that I was describing might have surprised her, but she understood the gravity of the situation quite well.

Our cooperation was very good and extremely valuable during that spring, but in those early days, the fact was that Sweden had started their process one step behind Finland. In both Sweden and Finland, there were also those who were hesitant to even discuss NATO for fear of causing an escalation in Europe. Bilateral and trilateral defense arrangements between Finland, Sweden, and the US were suggested as an alternative way for enhancing our countries' security. *Escalation* was the word on everyone's lips and some suggested we should "hold our horses."

After a press conference at Kesäranta, we convened at the headquarters of our Defense Command with President Niinistö and defense ministers from both countries. I described my take on the situation the same way, or even more frankly, as I had earlier with Prime Minister Andersson: the discussion on NATO membership would continue in Finland despite the fear of escalation, and it would be important to walk hand in hand with Sweden.

After the initial hesitation, things got rolling quickly. The decision to join NATO was not something we could reassess every year, or every four years; it would have to endure. Although it was my view that once Russia attacked Ukraine, Finland had no choice but to join NATO as soon as possible, we also had no choice but to do so as a united front. We needed to make sure that everyone was committed at every step of the way and that everyone involved in the decision-making felt they had access to all information available and had the opportunity to ask any questions. The process needed to be fast, but thorough. And it wasn't only important to build consensus in Finland but to do it together with Sweden. Every time we made a statement or decision, we made sure we were aligned and synchronized. The war meant we had to be very cautious about the optics of the situation; there was no room for loose opinions in the press or the appearance of discord—we couldn't give Russia any opportunities to intervene or to cause confusion.

Together with Charles Michel, Emmanuel Macron, the president of France, convened an informal meeting of the European Council in Versailles on March 10. From the meeting, we issued a declaration that summarized the situation: Russia's war of aggression constituted a tectonic shift in European history. We committed to bolstering our defense capabilities and to increasing defense spending. And we all agreed that a stronger and more capable EU would promote global and transatlantic security and would be a complement to NATO, which remained the foundation of collective defense for its members. There it was. Although the next line in the declaration confirmed "the solidarity between Member States" as stated in the EU Treaty's article 42(7), the cornerstone for security was NATO.

As we convened upstairs, my advisors stepped aside to meet with Prime Minister Andersson's two state secretaries. Speaking in confidence among fellow Social Democrats, my advisors told them that the process in Finland—in the Social Democratic Party but also among other parties—was likely to be fast, and it was vital that the Swedes move at the same pace. None of the other alternatives—bilateral or multilateral arrangements—were really options here. If there were conflicting messages from the meetings in Helsinki a week earlier, we hoped to deliver a clear indication of where we were heading.

Through March, April, and May, we maintained daily contact with EU and NATO countries: aiming to ensure we had support when we submitted our application. Federal Chancellor Olaf Scholz of Germany voiced his support in bilateral talks in Berlin a few days after our informal European Council meeting at the Palace of Versailles. I met Canadian Prime Minister Justin Trudeau in Brussels, Greek Prime Minister Kyriakos Mitsotakis in Athens, German Federal President Frank-Walter Steinmeier in Helsinki, Italian Prime Minister Mario Draghi in Rome, and the prime ministers of Norway, Denmark, and Iceland in Copenhagen. At the same time, we kept up discussions with Great Britain and France. In March, President Biden arrived at the European Council in Brussels to discuss transatlantic partners' support for Ukraine.

At the beginning of April, my advisors drafted a plan outlining when we needed decisions on applying for NATO membership, both from my own party and from the other parties in government. We wanted to make rapid progress during the spring, and our focus was once again joint decision-making with Sweden. We needed to talk to Prime Minister Andersson. I asked my advisors to arrange a visit to Stockholm as soon as possible.

Sunny spring weather greeted us when we landed in Stockholm on April 13. Andersson met me in front of the beautiful Villa Bonnier, and we walked alone along the waterfront path. As we moved inside to have lunch together with the Swedish foreign minister and a small team of advisors, we locked our phones away so that our discussion—coordinating the NATO process between our countries and the next concrete steps—couldn't be followed. I explained that the majority of members of parliament in Finland had already declared their support for membership, even publicly. I told Andersson that when the time was right for my party, I would announce that I was in favor of membership so that we could keep close to the timeline. Andersson and her minister referred to their own internal discussion, which they said would take time because of their long tradition of neutrality. But we agreed on the strategic importance of the membership of both countries. So eventually, counting the days we both needed, we found a common vision of the timeline for the next few weeks.

As my advisors and I moved to the Finnish embassy to meet the Finnish press, we realized that the visit had served its purpose—the Swedish Social Democrats were going to speed up. The strategic objective—to announce that both countries were applying for NATO membership simultaneously—was within reach.

# 8.

# GEOPOLITICAL REALITIES

**I had been to Ukraine only once before** the war began. In 2008, when I was twenty-two years old, I attended a progressive youth conference organized by the organization YES, or Yalta European Strategy. The conference brought about two hundred young politicians and representatives of different youth organizations to the capital, Kyiv, to discuss Ukraine's possible accession to the EU, democracy, and the country's future more broadly. For me, the gathering was an introduction to how international cooperation between parties from various political backgrounds might work.

The conference was also an introduction to Ukraine: its people, politics, culture, and art. I still remember talking with locals in the city center during that weekend—people were using the streets for gatherings and as a big marketplace, as they were closed from cars. I always thought of my short time there fondly. And I never expected that my next visit would take place under such dismal circumstances.

At the end of May 2022, the war had been raging for three months when I arrived at the Kyiv train station with my foreign policy advisor Lauri Voionmaa and my security team. The atmosphere was tense, and we were given careful instructions about safety protocols. We couldn't wear seatbelts in case we needed to quickly exit the vehicle if it was hit; we heard detailed descriptions of what to do if there was an air strike. No one could bring their regular phones, or any other devices that could be surveilled. I had a bulletproof vest and a secure travel phone with me. It was my first time visiting a war zone. Still, I wasn't afraid. It was part of the job.

When the war started, there was a general worry that the Russian army would reach Kyiv within days or weeks to overthrow the government. But Ukraine had managed to hold them off much more effectively than most had predicted. The US and UK had helped train Ukrainian soldiers and provided military equipment to the country prior to the war, and as a result Ukraine was more prepared to defend itself than it had been in 2014, when Russia invaded and annexed Crimea. Meanwhile, Russia was not as capable as we'd thought. They were using old tactics and clearly had not been expecting such fierce resistance from the Ukrainians. It became evident that the Ukrainian army was dedicated and prepared, and would not give up.

Not many people knew about my visit to Kyiv beforehand, and

it was planned on a tight timetable. Among the few back home who knew about my visit were the president and foreign minister, the four other leaders of the government, and my family, who were very worried about my safety. The details were only distributed to a handful of people because we wanted to make sure the trip would be as safe as possible. It was especially important that the media did not know I was traveling to Kyiv before I arrived, to prevent any interference in the trip. We would have a press conference with President Zelensky once we got there.

I have visited Ukraine many times since February 2022, and each time I have taken the overnight train. It takes more than a day to get there even though the distance to Kyiv is roughly the same as traveling to Lapland from Helsinki—just over a two-hour plane flight. The first train journey has stayed in my mind because the mood was so grave. The windows were covered so that no one passing the train could see who was inside—and to make the train less noticeable from the air as it made its way across the country. Throughout the night, whenever we would hear a noise, our imagination would go into overdrive: Was that gunfire? It was something I'd never experienced before. I was happy to get some sleep eventually because I would be working from early morning until late the next night.

The first stops on our visit were Irpin and Bucha, the cities outside Kyiv where Russian soldiers had tortured and murdered hundreds of innocent people and destroyed civilian infrastructure at the beginning of the war. Standing at the site of mass graves at the orthodox church of St. Andrew the Apostle in Bucha, I felt deep sadness and powerlessness in the face of all that cruelty. I fought back tears and tried to stay as composed as possible. Seeing the devastation and talking to residents about what they'd experienced made a lasting impression on me. It placed all the meetings and talks and sanctions into stark relief. If I was determined before to provide any help we could to Ukraine, I was even more so after this visit.

Driving to Kyiv, we had to avoid blockades, as well as bridges the Ukrainian army had demolished as a defense strategy to prevent Russian troops getting closer to the capital. As soon as we arrived in the city, we met with the Finnish ambassador to Ukraine and continued on our way to meet the speaker of the Ukrainian parliament. Our ambassador, like all essential personnel, had had to leave Kyiv in the aftermath of the Russian full-scale invasion, but she had returned before my arrival. After the talks with the speaker of parliament, we traveled to a government building to meet with President Zelensky and Prime Minister Denys Shmyhal. Security was very tight—the building was lined with sandbags both inside and out to shield windows and absorb some of the impact if the building was attacked. Soldiers guided us to the meeting room using flashlights in otherwise dark corridors.

President Zelensky had participated in European Council meetings remotely that spring, so this was only the second time that I'd met with him face to face. The first time was in Brussels the previous December during the Eastern Partnership summit. This time we discussed what Finland and the EU could do to continue supporting the war effort, with arms, financial support, and humanitarian aid, as well as sanctions. He was focused, calm, and determined, and even though he must have been tired, he did not show it. I felt empathy toward him: first a pandemic, then war, and also Russia's constant attempts on his life. It is an unthinkable burden for any person to carry. But even though the mood in Ukraine was very somber, I received a warm welcome, and it was evident Finnish support was valued highly in the country. I had been a vocal and straightforward leader commenting on Russia's actions in Ukraine. Ukraine also kept a close watch on our NATO process and supported us.

After we left the government building, we were able to see what was going on in Kyiv. As always, I preferred walking. What we saw on foot made a much bigger impression on us than it would have from a car window. Despite the war and danger, Ukrainians were living their lives as normally as possible: they were in cafés and parks, they were going to the grocery store, they were taking their children to the playground. Quickly I began to feel uneasy, almost rude, wearing my bulletproof vest. These people were living their lives every day in the middle of war and did not wear any safety gear. So after talking about it with the local security team, I decided to take off my vest and continued to walk and talk with locals. Afterward, we left for the train station, where we took the same night train back to Poland before traveling home to Finland the next morning.

Since the trip I have met Zelensky many times: in Ukraine, at different European meetings, and in Finland. I have come to value him not only as a leader but as a person. He is always admirably frank; he is as brave in personal conversations as he is in public. I remember the time he visited Helsinki in May 2023 especially warmly. Emma, who was five years old at the time, joined me at the Presidential Palace that day because I'd had problems arranging a babysitter. Even at her age, Emma was aware of the situation in Ukraine, and she was excited to meet Zelensky. During our discussion, Emma wandered around the palace with my advisor and one of the president's aides-de-camp and, apparently, secretly picked a flower from some flower arrangement. After our meeting she came into the room and handed the flower to President Zelensky. A father himself, he received the gift with a smile. He was much more at ease that day than when we met in Kyiv the year before.

○

Because of the war and our NATO process, my travel schedule was packed in 2022. A few days after my trip to Ukraine, I went to Brussels to a European Council meeting; a few days after that I flew to Washington, D.C., to a Bilderberg meeting that also gave me an opportunity to meet with the secretary general of NATO, Jens Stoltenberg, and with Speaker of the House Nancy Pelosi. The trip to D.C. ended up giving me a moment of rest, but not for a pleasant reason. Traveling back via London I got COVID for the first time. Heathrow Airport was full of people, there were no safety protocols in place anymore, and we had to wait several hours for our connecting flight to Finland. After landing in Helsinki, my first couple of at-home COVID tests were negative, but within a few days I started to feel unusually tired and my temperature rose rapidly, so I took another test: positive. I would have to quarantine and could only work remotely.

Except for this brief enforced pause, I was very busy. On top of meeting with visitors who came to Helsinki, and of course the rest of the job, I made over thirty visits to foreign countries in 2022. There is a structured procedure for nations seeking to join NATO, which includes unanimous approval from the member countries.

We wanted to make sure Finland could count on their support once we officially applied. Part of these discussions was dedicated to ensuring each country would support ratifying our application as soon as possible, as well as ratifying that of Sweden. I also traveled to countries that are NATO partners but not official members, to discuss the situation in Ukraine and Europe, and our discourse concerning the alliance.

I especially remember my visit to Tokyo. The trip itself was a success, and my delegation and I had a very good conversation with the Japanese prime minister, Fumio Kishida, about geopolitics and NATO as well as Finland and Japan's relations. The only problem was that I was so jet-lagged that I stayed awake for days. Finally all the international travel had caught up to me. Although I am usually an excellent sleeper—I could even sleep on the train to Ukraine and, once, in a helicopter visiting the Åland Islands—my trip to Japan, which took place just a few weeks before the trip to Ukraine in May 2022, taught me never to take that skill for granted. I ended up staying awake for almost fifty hours straight. I remember just lying in bed, thinking about how horrible I felt—how it didn't seem possible that I was so tired and yet couldn't sleep, and how much worse I was going to feel. The next day, the schedule was once again packed; there was no time to be tired. One of the most important events of the trip—a dinner with Prime Minister Kishida—was that evening.

I was nauseated with exhaustion, and worried about how I would perform at dinner. But as soon as we arrived, I forgot all about how little I had slept. The dinner itself was beautiful and thoughtfully organized—the entire meal, for the whole party, was vegetarian, to

the Partnership for Peace in 1994. They also gave us credit for our defense forces, which could rely on a very large and trained reserve. We received a warm welcome for our application. In the end, only two countries were hesitant: Turkey and Hungary. And it was about politics as usual.

The main problem was Turkey, and not with us, but with Sweden. There have been several speculations about President Erdoğan's motives. Officially, Turkey claimed Sweden had weak anti-terrorism legislation: some Kurdish minority groups in Sweden are labeled as terrorists in Turkey, and the two countries have had strained relations. My assessment is that the real reasons for the delay in ratification were political; President Erdoğan used the opportunity to leverage the NATO process to influence totally separate negotiations to buy a fleet of fighter jets from the US, as well as to affect an election that was coming up in Turkey.

At the Munich Security Conference in 2023, my delegation and I, along with the Swedish Prime Minister Ulf Kristersson, successor to Magdalena Andersson, met with Vice President Kamala Harris to discuss our NATO process and European security more broadly. During our meeting, I asked what kind of side talks the US was having with Turkey concerning the fighter jets and how they would ensure our applications move forward. It was evident the frank question made the vice president uneasy. And it was understandable—the situation was difficult for the US. I said to both Swedish prime ministers, first Andersson and later to Kristersson, that it wasn't wise to agree to every demand Erdoğan had because Turkey would only ask for more, which they did several times. Both Finland and Sweden were fully qualified to be NATO members, and hewing resolutely to the facts of the case would give negotiators a stronger position in the long run. My certainty only grew when I discussed the situation with the Hungarian prime minister, Viktor Orbán, and President Erdoğan. I spoke to Orbán many times on the sidelines of European Council meetings, and he always had the same thing to say: Hungary would ratify our bid eventually, once Turkey moved forward; there were no specific problems with us. I still think he also wanted to keep the door open to leverage the talks for something else. I only spoke with Erdoğan once as his official counterpart was our president—it was during the European Political Community Summit in Prague in October 2022. I expected a difficult discussion, but it was the opposite. He said to me that Turkey had no problem with Finland and that they would ratify our bid when the time was right. His presence was very friendly, and he spoke to me with a noticeably gentle tone. When I asked what the problem was, his answer was simple: Sweden. It was evident that Turkey wanted to separate our ratification processes, and in the end they were successful. Finland joined NATO on April 4, 2023, in the fastest accession processes of all time; Sweden became a member almost a year after, on March 7, 2024. And Erdoğan won the Turkish elections and got the fighter jets. Well played.

In the end, the fact that two new countries joined NATO was a major victory for the alliance and a huge loss to Russia, which has stated its goal to prevent NATO's eastern expansion. But the process also showed weaknesses in NATO itself. If it was that easy to sidetrack negotiations with countries that fulfill all the criteria, it suggests that unanimity is hard to come by, and because all NATO decisions require agreement, it puts leadership in a difficult spot.

○

Just before Finland joined NATO, in March 2023, I made another trip to Ukraine. The first time I visited as prime minister, not many European leaders had been to Ukraine during the war. But because of Finland's geography, strong support to Ukraine, and the fact that we were embarking on the NATO process at the time, I wanted to be there relatively early during the conflict.

By the time I returned to the country in 2023, the situation had become more stable. The trip was not nearly as momentous; security protocols were looser. I met Zelensky outside, and we entered the government building together. The main subject on the table was the material help and air defense capabilities that Ukraine desperately needed. Zelensky asked if Finland could provide fighter jets, and I replied that although I couldn't promise him anything, we would discuss the matter. We had already made the significant decision to purchase F-35 fighter jets from the United States, meaning that our old fleet of F-18 Hornets would be replaced in the coming years.

Much of the schedule on that second trip to Ukraine as a prime minister was dedicated to understanding how the country was faring on the ground. Human rights had deteriorated ever since Russia started the extensive violence against the civilian population, and I spoke with human rights lawyers and representatives from human rights organizations about the widespread abuses and war crimes: in addition to attacks on energy infrastructure, hospitals, schools, train stations, and other civilian buildings, murder, rape, torture, and the abduction of Ukrainian children to Russia were systematically conducted. The use of land mines made everyday life extremely danger-ous, and made the land unusable for farming, as well.

One of the lighter moments of the trip was when we visited a school that focused on athletics in the partially rebuilt town of Bucha, where I had seen mass graves just a year earlier. Because I had got-ten into playing basketball at the prime minister's residence during COVID, I shot some hoops with the students there. It was so uplift-ing seeing kids on the playground. This was where they should be: in school, not in a war zone. We also visited a hospital in Kyiv to talk to injured soldiers, and met with hospital staff, nurses, and doctors to discuss what they needed and how we could help. We announced a humanitarian aid package designated for education, environment, and enhancing radiation safety.

Although morale among citizens was good, or as good as it can be during such a conflict, the reality of war was omnipresent. As time goes on during war, people get tired—not only of the war ef-fort and the fighting, but of the constant stress and insecurity. An air-raid siren can go off at any moment; a spouse or a parent could die in battle or be taken as a prisoner of war. Even as Ukrainians continue to live their lives, taking their children to school, buying groceries, and going to cafés and bars and clubs, they know that the makeshift stability they have built for themselves could collapse at any moment. But I have not met or talked to anyone from Ukraine who says they'll give up.

As the war has dragged on, new false narratives have begun to proliferate suggesting that the Ukrainian people do not want to fight for themselves anymore, and there have been arguments stating that Europe and the United States are prolonging the suffering by sending more weapons. This is not true, of course, but has gained some traction among people who don't want to support Ukraine, or who are just tired of everything the war has brought to our lives: high energy prices, inflation, increasing insecurity. The face of the war is extremely brutal, and Ukrainians are paying a heavy price defending not only their own land but the democratic values that we believe in. But I suspect this disturbing narrative that flips the responsibility of the war to the West is orchestrated and supported by Russia.

In my view, this war is not just about Ukraine and Russia, and it is vitally important that the West not cave to defeatist thinking. The implications of a Russian victory are catastrophic, and would reach far beyond Lviv and the Donbas.

○

One question that many analysts—and civilians—have asked is how we got to this point. After the collapse of the Soviet Union and the end of the Cold War many Western countries became complacent with the idea that liberal democracy and capitalism had prevailed and the great ideological struggle was resolved. The decades that followed were an optimistic time. Many believed global trade and democratic values were spreading successfully, also within Russia.

After Putin was first elected prime minister in 1999, Russian society began to change again. He grew the economy while also leading military campaigns against Chechen separatists, attacking Georgia, annexing Crimea, and intervening in the Syrian war. At the same time, hostile changes in Russian society were gradually becoming apparent. Opposition to Putin's regime was increasingly silenced, often violently, and anti-LGBTQ legislation began to ring alarm bells within human rights groups.

But the West did not respond; it did not take the threats represented by Putin's increasingly draconian domestic legislation and violently expansionist foreign policy seriously enough. In 2014 after Russia invaded Crimea, the response was near silence. Although Western countries established sanctions against Russia at that time, no policy operated as a genuine deterrent. Many leaders continued to believe in the stabilizing effect of economic interdependence—that it would simply be too expensive for Russia not to follow our rules. We also wanted to maintain trade with Russia, and particularly to retain our access to their cheap energy sources. Even as opponents of the regime, most famously the opposition leader and activist Alexei Navalny, were poisoned, stalked, and imprisoned, the West did not counter Russia's crimes with strength or conviction.

So while the full-scale invasion of Ukraine was certainly a shock to the West, and it was certainly unbelievable from our perspective and logic, it did not come out of nowhere. Russia took advantage of the West's prior indifference, or denial, to launch their invasion. I don't believe Russia would have done so if Western societies had passed the test Russia was administering in 2014. The reaction to the invasion of Crimea was so weak that the country felt comfortable straying further and further from rules-based international order.

Through its aggression, Russia has broken and abandoned some of the key principles and commitments of the European security system. This is the reality we will be facing even when the war is over. In order to avoid the mistakes we have made in the past, we have to update our understanding of the reasoning and logic that Russia, as well as other authoritarian regimes, follow; prioritizing power and respect over economic growth. This is why the quality of the peace, and what comes after, is as important as the cessation of war. If Russia gains land and other victories in Ukraine, their will to expand will only grow stronger. Gray zones and frozen conflicts, rather than stable peace, will proliferate, heating up again and again as aggression continues on European soil.

Unfortunately, it's not just Russia's logic Western powers have failed to understand and to prepare for. Only recently have Western leaders begun to discuss the authoritarian mindset as a contemporary issue, not a relic of history. With China, we have already seen crackdowns on human rights in Hong Kong and pressure on Taiwan, as well as severe human rights violations against minorities such as the Uyghur people in the west of the country. All the while, the West has looked the other way, as it has not been in our immediate interest to face the brutal reality.

Just as Europe's dependence on Russian energy created a huge problem when Russia sought to use those resources as leverage, Western reliance on Chinese natural resources, and especially on its technology manufacturing infrastructure, is a huge weakness for our economies. We are trading convenience and low costs now for a future in which we may depend on a country that does not share our values. The West has been so afraid of losing access to cheap fossil energy and the factories we use to produce the goods our citizens use and our companies sell that we have lost sight of the bigger picture:

defending our values and the rules-based international order. From the perspective of a smaller country like Finland, a future without shared rules, in which nations can rely only on strength and power, is frightening.

Our economic reliance on regimes that do not share our values will only give those regimes the space to exert pressure on our countries, and our economies, in the future. The foreign policy we see as pragmatism has a heavier cost than we realize. If the European Union and Western countries do not build strategic autonomy with trusted partners in critical areas such as energy, natural resources, medicines and medical equipment, defense capabilities, and technology, we will find ourselves in a situation in which we can be blackmailed. We will descend into a culture of self-censorship out of fear of the consequences.

But there is a silver lining; the tense geopolitical situation is now giving us an opportunity to identify our weaknesses, and to change.

Europe must send a clear message: acts of aggression and oppression will not result in false compromises with authoritarian regimes. We must make it clear that expansionism and authoritarianism will only lead to a more integrated European continent that is united in a shared respect for peace, stability, and international law, as well as by a belief in the right of sovereign nations to chart their own futures. To defend these values, we must accept that difficult times are coming and prepare for them. We must strengthen our relations with democratic partners in Asia, the Indo-Pacific region, and the global South. We need to strengthen trade with countries that share our values and develop technological innovations collectively. And we need to strengthen our own military forces and capabilities fast, especially now when the US has indicated very clearly that Europe can't rely on its presence in the future. We were not as prepared as we could have been for the Russian invasion of Ukraine, and we need to accept the lesson that experience taught us. This isn't theoretical—it will happen again. When it does, we need to be ready.

# 9.

# TOUGH NEGOTIATIONS

**Joining NATO may have been** one of the most difficult, multifaceted processes I went through as prime minister—and it came directly on the heels of endless COVID decisions, too. But reaching results on many other issues required just as much skill, knowledge, strategy, conviction, and endurance. To be able to negotiate effectively requires an understanding of how different outcomes might affect other negotiations, and the ability to see (at least) two steps ahead. The mood of negotiations, and your own behavior, leave a mark on others that may affect your ability to get what you want, or need, in the future. I find that the hardest part of navigating negotiations isn't understanding what outcomes will result from different scenarios, but understanding how to walk the path to a solution together with others so that they feel seen and understood. If people don't feel that they really participated, they don't feel ownership of the outcome and aren't committed to what follows.

If Finland's unity on the NATO process emerged from the dire circumstances Russia created by invading Ukraine, other issues came with more room, and time, for debate. From the very beginning of my term, when we negotiated the repatriation of Finnish citizens from the al-Hol refugee camp, and then almost immediately began to deal with the daily crisis that was the COVID-19 pandemic, the five women leaders of government got together almost every week, and sometimes even every day, to discuss and negotiate whatever was on the agenda. My term as a member of parliament was instructive on how to adapt my personality to work with very different people, but the negotiations during my term as prime minister were of a different order, and not only because I was operating at the top level of the government. The number of crises, as well as the government's ambitious program, meant that the pace of negotiations was particularly intense. Because the program included so many reforms and policies from our party's platform, we were very invested in the outcomes of every negotiation. The SDP was finally determining the direction of politics, and the turmoil surrounding Antti Rinne's resignation and my appointment meant the stakes were especially high.

These negotiations took place on the national level as well as within the EU, and as with NATO, complications often arose when we had to integrate the two levels. In the European Union the twenty-seven member states and their leaders are constantly dealing with their own particular national circumstances—everyday politics, preparing for elections, and handling crises and scandals—and at the same time dealing with wider European issues and trying to find solutions and compromises on common problems. Every country has their own specific interests and cultural and political realities that sometimes collide with those of the others. From the outside, EU negotiations—and especially the work of the European Council—might look slow and inefficient, a matter of simply making compromises upon compromises. And many times it *is* like this. But during the last few years, the proliferation of crises has meant the EU had to come together and make unprecedented decisions, shaping the future of the entire continent. Often the hardest situations force us to re-evaluate and reform structures, and this has been the case for the EU.

One of the most time-consuming and demanding negotiations in the European Union is the process of agreeing on the budget framework and policy programs for a seven-year period. Again, this may sound dull and bureaucratic, but it can be quite intense. Because Finland happened to hold the rotating presidency of the EU when this came around for the years 2021–2027, we were responsible for negotiating with all member states on the basis of the European Commission's proposal of what's known as the Multiannual Financial Framework (MFF). However, the conditions of these negotiations are important to understand. The budget agreement is only finalized at the very last minute by the leaders at the European Council. Before this the process drags on for about two years. Proposals are made and then rejected, over and over. When the president of the European Council, Charles Michel, called a summit in February 2020, hopes weren't high for an agreement—it was far too early for anyone to show enough willingness to compromise. During the meeting, Michel and the president of the European Commission, Ursula von der Leyen, invited every member state to meetings on the top floor of the council's building. Because Finland had been the last country to hold the presidency, my advisors and I were the last group to enter the room—it was about 6 a.m., following a long day and night of talks. We found Michel and von der Leyen both half-asleep with a couple of key officials. There was no chance of an agreement—we could have told them so earlier. With help from our excellent team of financial experts, we knew that the proposal on the table was far from what we, or any other member state, would be willing to accept. And once we collected our notes and everyone left Brussels, we still didn't know that COVID would radically change the entire economic landscape.

Several months later, in July 2020, the European Council met again to negotiate over the MFF for the bloc. The pandemic had had dramatic consequences for the economy all over Europe. Negotiating the MFF is always tricky, but this time it was even more complicated. Given that we were still in the thick of COVID, the framework would now include the Next Generation EU Temporary Recovery and Resilience Facility instrument, which at the time totaled 750 billion euros in grants and loans for member states to support reforms and investments, in addition to funding for long-term EU priorities such as green and digital transitions. From an economic perspective, this was a major moment in history; there was a serious risk of a downturn in the European economy, and of rising interest rates that would drive some EU countries into very difficult financial situations because of how much debt they had. Finland is a net payer member state within the EU, meaning that we provide more money than we receive from the bloc, so the instrument itself wasn't that beneficial to us. But as a small, export-driven country operating in the European single market, we were certainly very invested in the overall economic situation. What's more, many EU countries, Finland included, would simply be too small to compete economically, and maintain security, without the support of a broader network. The entire system is based on solidarity and the principle of filling gaps between countries.

Finland's concerns were to do with the recovery instrument, not only the amount itself, but the concept in principle. The Finnish constitution says that the mandate to handle the budget belongs to parliament, and parliament's Constitutional Committee was concerned that funding the instrument through the EU's joint debt—and especially using it to fund grants to member states—would undermine the Finnish parliament's budgetary power, transferring some of its mandate to the EU. In other words, the way the recovery instrument was funded started a debate in the committee about whether it would need to be approved in the Finnish parliament with a supermajority—two-thirds of voting members—when the EU's own Resources Decision, including the instrument, would be given to national parliaments for ratification.

For me, this meant that I would need support not only from the parliamentary groups in my government, but also from the opposition, to make sure the budget agreement held in our parliament. This was an extra complication that I didn't need when entering the MFF negotiations in July 2020, which were already extremely complicated. In Finland, the prime minister leads EU policy, but the whole government negotiates and agrees on these matters together in a ministerial committee on EU affairs. The number of issues that fall under the umbrella of EU policy is so large that all ministries are practically in charge of their own area, but what makes the Finnish model unique is how we coordinate EU legislation and decision-making. A "Grand Committee" in parliament has the broad right to receive information about EU affairs and participate in creating guidelines concerning decision-making within the EU. This means that all ministers, including the prime minister, are required to have hearings in parliament both before and after council meetings in the EU. During the negotiations, I was in regular contact with the committee chair Satu Hassi—a very experienced politician who, fortunately, understood the realities of negotiations of this scale.

In the July MFF negotiations in Brussels, I had two main objectives. First was to make sure that the framework budget for 2021–2027 was moderate, and that our priorities would be covered. The second was to limit the recovery instrument, especially the amount of grants, and to ensure that the legal questions were clarified and the instrument would be precisely defined. The commission's initial proposal was to issue two-thirds of the recovery in grants, and only one-third in loans; we wanted the distribution to be more balanced. Alongside these two main objectives, it was important to Finland that any country receiving EU budget money was required to abide by the rule of law—meaning that flouting the rule of law would lead a country to lose its EU funding.

We weren't alone in our concerns. Other so-called "frugal" countries—Austria, Denmark, the Netherlands, and Sweden—were also opposed to issuing so many grants and we worked closely together. As another major net payer, Germany had usually aligned with frugal countries in MFF negotiations. But Angela Merkel, who was still chancellor at the time, had given the commission the green light, alongside the French president, Emmanuel Macron, to propose a recovery instrument without consulting the other frugal countries. Several leaders were disappointed, and even personally hurt, by this; the countries had relied on Merkel to keep them informed.

The Finnish government had stated quite clearly that Finland wouldn't accept the recovery instrument as it was proposed, so I had to be extremely firm on demanding changes. I was also concerned that the outcome might not pass our parliament if it needed to be approved with a two-thirds majority later. At the time, we didn't know how the Constitutional Committee would interpret the requirements, but it was evident that the issue had already been highly politicized within the committee.

The July negotiations in the European Council lasted five days, which always stretched to night sessions. I often slept on the couch of our delegation room during the bilateral meetings between Michel and von der Leyen and other member states, just to be able to continue negotiating. In these kinds of negotiations, there are always the official negotiations and then negotiations between different member states in different formats. Because of Finland's misgivings about the recovery instrument, I was on all the key tables. We also helped other member states to understand the "NegoBox"—Brussels shorthand for "negotiating box," a document that holds the information of the framework—as we had presented it the previous fall and knew all the figures it contained. As the negotiations proceed further, the Nego-Box changes and it becomes hard to track. Huddled in a basement of the government building in Finland, with a 24/7 video link to our quarters in the council, our experts were able to track all the major shifts within the box. At one point, the Finnish delegation offered help that was even more practical: the copy machine in the German delegation office had broken, and an official ran to our offices to plead for help—Chancellor Merkel needed a copy right away. Luckily two of my advisors had just been able to fix our own broken machine, and the chancellor got what she needed.

The Finnish delegation room is located next to Germany's, which meant it was also proximate to many of the secondary negotiations moderated by Merkel, who was trying to find compromises among the twenty-seven member states. In addition to hoping to cut down the amount of money allocated to grants, which was a concern I shared with the other leaders of frugal countries, the conditions attached to receiving this funding remained important to me. In particular, the stipulation that all recipients adhere to the rule of law was very important. Finland and many other member states and EU institutions had become very worried about the erosion of the rule of law in Hungary under Viktor Orbán's rule. It was time to start using what seemed to be the most effective means to influence the situation: money.

As the negotiations were slowly coming to an end, I sat at the same table with Orbán, Merkel, von der Leyen, and a few other leaders, trying to find a solution to the rule of law mechanism. Much of the package had been settled—the frugal countries were able to move 110 billion euros from grants to loans—but Hungary refused to sign the budget if the rule of law stipulation was in place. Merkel had tried for hours to bridge a compromise, but what they could get Hungary to agree with wasn't enough for me and Stefan Löfven, the prime minister of Sweden at the time. After a while, they decided to invite us into the negotiation room as well. After a long drafting session we came to an agreement Hungary could accept, and then we took a quick break so that our experts could confirm that the language was robust enough to make an actual difference. It was a crucial victory that we were able to link the rule of law mechanism to the use of EU funds. Today, the EU still withholds funds from Hungary because of their rule of law violations.

Even though I worked side by side with "the frugals," Finland wasn't officially part of this group as our interests differed on some issues, mainly the distribution of agricultural funds. On our specific interests in agriculture policy and rural development or cohesion programs, I worked together with countries like Poland, Portugal, and Bulgaria. This familiarity ultimately helped me in the final push. In negotiations that have a lot of moving pieces, it is important to know all the other players' main priorities so that you can form alignments strategically. Because I was at so many different negotiating tables, I tried to make sure that everything Finland wanted was also supported by other parties so that our priorities had momentum.

In the end, when the conclusions from the meeting were almost finalized, and all our other key priorities were tackled, it was time for my last demand. Since all European Council proposals need to be agreed upon unanimously, there is always some room for member states to advocate for specific needs, especially at the end of negotiations when everyone just wants to be finished. To put it another way: there is some room to buy countries to back the overall deal.

Because Finland was opposed in principle to direct grants instead of loans, I could use the political repercussions I'd face at home for the subsidy program to justify getting more money from the budget. I wanted "an envelope"—money especially allocated to Finland—in the amount of 500 million euros. Because we knew the NegoBox so well and tracked its changes as the negotiations proceeded, I had made sure that the programs like rural development funds had room to allocate some of this money to us. And Finland happened to have some rural development needs.

The 500 million Finland needed was relatively insignificant in the context of the total cost of the MFF and recovery instrument: 1.8 trillion euros. But to Finland it was very important. As the negotiations dragged on and on, Charles Michel began to get irritated trying to come up with a proposal that would be accepted by all twenty-seven member states. One morning he called me at my hotel to try to convince me to agree to the terms being proposed at the time. In exchange for my cooperation, he said he'd give me an envelope—of 150 million euros. I told him I wouldn't accept any deal unless Finland received 500 million euros for rural development and special support for sparsely populated areas in northern and eastern Finland.

Michel was absolutely furious: he hung up.

In the European context, Finland is a small country, and we can't simply make demands or dictate what we need. Instead, we have to be strategic and clever in building alliances with larger countries and using their leverage in negotiations. And nobody had the experience and leverage like Angela Merkel, who was always in the center of every deal.

After this angry phone call with Michel, I found myself in another meeting with Merkel. I told her that it was good that the negotiations were going in the direction of approving the rule of law stipulation and other key issues for us, but that I had a problem. I told her about the difficulties we might face in parliament for the final approval of the proposal if the Constitutional Committee ruled that we needed a supermajority to go ahead. I told her I was also worried about how it would look if we couldn't secure a good deal for Finland—I couldn't go back home empty-handed. I needed a big envelope to show that Finland would benefit from the outcome of the negotiations, even if the final proposal held on to things that we didn't like.

Merkel understood immediately: Of course, she said, I couldn't go home without an envelope. And then she told one of her advisors to handle it.

Within a few hours, Charles Michel came to me, very cooperative, and told me Finland would get its 500-million-euro envelope.

Nobody had thought we could get an envelope this size. When I returned to Finland, it was treated as a major win. Even the Center Party, traditionally very difficult to please, was happy.

It was always evident that Finland couldn't dictate whether there should be a recovery instrument once the big players like Germany and France had approved the proposal. It also became clear, in retrospect, that approving the funding was an important reason we didn't have a bigger economic crisis in Europe. Still, we were able to channel the negotiations in ways that were highly important for us: we made gains in terms of our principles and in terms of our bottom line.

But the negotiations weren't over for Finland yet. The following spring, after the European negotiations concluded, Finland's Constitutional Committee ruled that the decision needed to be ratified with a supermajority from our parliament—the outcome we had worried about, because it would depend on the government getting at least some approval from the opposition. This part of the story was highly politicized in Finland, but because the deal I had negotiated for us the previous year was good enough, we got the votes we needed. If Finland had voted against the agreement, it would have been a catastrophe for the EU and our status within the bloc. Negotiations would have had to start all over again, and because we would have been the ones to cause more headache and stress, Finland would have been expected to present a better proposal. At times, my job felt like navigating a minefield, trying to dismantle potential problems before they exploded. Because I had always tried to stay two steps ahead of the discussions, I was able to balance our priorities alongside the collective's goals.

○

It won't be surprising to hear that budget negotiations are often tense. The EU budget was a beast, but in fall 2020 we also had a difficult set of talks closer to home during our own budget negotiations. Although these should have been more straightforward, it's sometimes the smaller problems that become sticking points. The issue on the table was peat, the material similar to soil that is produced by the decomposition of organic matter in wet, acidic environments like bogs and swamps. Bogs are common in cold, wet climates like Finland's, and swamps and marshlands make up about one-third of our landscape. We have extracted and burned peat for energy for a long time, along with the rest of our diverse energy mix.

Although bogs are vital to the earth's natural carbon cycle—they have absorbed a lot of carbon from the atmosphere in their lifetime and function as carbon storages—many countries use peat as energy. This is extremely environmentally unfriendly. It's even worse than burning coal, in terms of climate emissions. Peat is also not renewable, so while the marshlands that produce it are vital to biodiversity and the overall health of an ecosystem, restoring depleted bogs and swamps can take decades or even hundreds of years.

Nevertheless, for decades there have been compelling arguments to continue using peat to maintain our relative self-sufficiency—an independence that proved important when Russia declared war in Ukraine. Ideally, we would reserve the use of it for true disaster situations, when other energy sources are no longer available, and otherwise do what's best for the climate and environment by eliminating it from our normal energy mix. For the SDP, it was clear that in the coming years we would have to give up burning peat, as long as we could do it in a manner that would be socially just and fair—securing jobs and livelihood for people that are working within the industry.

Peat was particularly important to two parties in our government: the Greens, for obvious reasons, and the Center Party, because of their background and interests in agriculture. Most of their voters come from rural areas, and many work in fields related to agriculture. For many Center Party supporters, peat was a symbolic issue: the push to eliminate peat was an example of urban elites controlling their way of life. The two parties occupied totally opposite sides on the issue, and as happened in many negotiations, the SDP was caught in the middle. Climate and labor are both core issues in our platform; pursuing climate targets without creating unbearable situations for people was important to us.

As prime minister, it was my task to find a compromise on the issue between the five parties in government. I also happened to know something about peat because I'd led the table that handled climate and environmental issues when we negotiated the governmental program, and peat was among the hardest issues to deal with at the time.

In the 2020 budget talks, once everything else had been solved, including other climate and energy questions, peat was haunting us once again. Although it was a relatively minor issue compared to everything we'd decided, the peat discussions spun completely out of control. Every aspect of the issue seemed to come up for discussion, but the core question was about taxation. Historically, peat had been taxed at much lower rates than other heating fuels. The Ministry of Finance had proposed that it should be increased gradually in the upcoming years, but the Center Party was strictly against this. The Swedish People's Party was also critical of the proposal. The SDP, the Greens, and the Left Alliance were in favor, but it was our job to try to find the middle ground on this issue.

It would have been almost comical if it hadn't been so frustrating. Over and over, I presented compromises to the four parties, and every time I was met with rejection.

As ever, the political divide between those who focus on ideology and those who focus on strategy led to clashes. Parties that cater to a specific demographic—like the Swedish People's Party, or the Center Party with their base of farmers and people from rural areas—naturally tend to argue for specific things their voters want. More ideological and value-based parties, like the Greens and the Left Alliance, often have more abstract goals and need to maintain a certain image in order to win over voters who may not be as loyal to them as people who have very specific needs. The SDP is somewhere between the two poles—we are ideological and value-based, but with pragmatism and a long history in government, which means we are comfortable making compromises. Our dedication to workers' rights means we often have concrete policy goals that may seem disadvantageous to other areas (business, for example), but in this new era of policy reform, it was also important that we kept our core values and long-term vision in sight. On most issues, from climate to healthcare, we never really took an extreme or radical view compared to those on the fringes of the government. We understood that we didn't have a majority alone on any issue, so we were dedicated to compromise in order to accomplish our program. And we knew quite well which of our many objectives were the ones to really fight for.

On the surface, climate is one of the issues on which most of Finland is in relative agreement, or at least was at that time. In general, Finland has major advantages in passing climate policy that other countries might not have. There hasn't been such a polarized debate about whether Finland should do its part to fulfill the Paris Agreement, or whether the government should implement progressive climate policies. The discussion has been more about how progressive Finland should be and what concrete measures we should take to achieve our climate targets. Even our main industries have supported ambitious climate policy. We have a deep understanding of green and digital technologies and are able to see huge business potential in exporting climate-friendly solutions to international markets. It was always relatively easy to agree on our big climate targets—that Finland aims to be climate neutral by 2035 and net negative soon afterward, and that we should increase our research and development funding by up to 4 percent by 2030 in order to raise productivity. When we outlined our government program, thirteen industries laid out their own plans to contribute to the government's ambitious goals. Because we were able to get everyone involved, no one felt like they were being punished or unfairly treated, and usually, minor disagreements were easy to resolve because all parties felt like they were working toward a shared goal. For Finland, active climate policy is a matter of creating new jobs and maintaining competitiveness, and this view has been widely accepted and shared across our society.

Nevertheless, the devil is in the details. In my government, the Greens became somewhat fixated on pushing for tougher climate targets in order to demonstrate that they were the party most dedicated to climate. But during the reform of our party platform, the SDP also developed progressive climate policies. Because I'd focused on climate issues throughout my career, I had credibility on climate and the environment, and during the election we ended up taking some airtime—and voters—from the Greens. In an attempt to differentiate themselves on the issue, the Greens decided they had to be seen as even more aggressive than the SDP or the Left Alliance, who are also extremely committed to tough climate policy.

On the other side was the Center Party, which had debated internally over whether to join the government in the first place after their election defeat. They often struggled with their identity because they would make concessions to either the right or the left in order to be in government. Many of their parliamentarians wanted to join the opposition during the elections, but their leader at the time had convinced them to join, as it was more advantageous to be in government when defending their priorities. And one of these priorities was how peat should be taxed.

The SDP often tried to balance between the two parties—we were not always on the side of the Center Party or the Greens—because we needed both to have a majority in parliament. But on the peat issue, we clearly leaned toward the Greens. However, because the details on these proposals were often technical, some of the Greens were suspicious that they might contain loopholes they wouldn't like.

My priority in negotiations is always to reach an outcome at every step of the process. As a prime minister, I needed to be pragmatic and not lose sight of the big picture and what was at stake. But because peat became a symbolic issue, both sides exaggerated its significance, making a reasonable, big-picture discussion impossible. The fact is that peat isn't a sustainable heating fuel, and over time we will abandon it except in emergencies. This will happen even without radical changes to tax policy, because of the EU Emissions Trading Scheme (ETS) that will increase its price, but it will happen faster if the tax is increased systematically. For me it was evident that the overall climate policy was more important than dismantling the government over small details.

Yet the debate went on and on. Once we had been stuck on the issue for hours, I decided to call my special advisor Matti Niemi, an advisor for EU affairs. Both Matti and I have a background working on climate and energy policy, but he has a unique ability to work toward compromise.

He picked up the phone. "Matti," I said, "you're on speakerphone. How can we solve this peat problem?"

All at once, everyone at the table started arguing, and almost shouting. All this, about peat! (At the time, it made up less than 5 percent of our energy mix). But I was losing my sense of humor as the negotiations were getting sidetracked. Everyone in the room was agitated. It was clear the problem was not going to be solved over the phone.

I asked Matti to come to the House of Estates to join the negotiations. It took him about half an hour to show up, and in the meantime, we worked on a plan. The solution was separate from taxation:

a price-floor mechanism that would prevent peat prices from sinking even if the emission allowance price dropped. It wasn't a totally new idea—it had been introduced in governmental negotiations one year before, and a similar model had been used on coal in the UK. The Center Party had turned it down back then, but maybe now was the time to reassess the proposal, because it wasn't as politicized as only using taxation as a tool. As Matti and I worked on the model, we also asked the chairman of the National Climate Panel to join the negotiations to evaluate how the mechanism would function. This was strategic: bringing a credible outside figure to the table would help the Greens trust us more. He was very helpful in convincing the Greens, and explaining to the Center Party how the model worked, so we were able to find a solution that was acceptable to the two parties that had been at each other's throats for days.

But I knew the issue would continue to torment us for the whole governmental term.

I wasn't wrong. One year later, in the 2021 budget negotiations, the Greens and the Center Party were again fighting over climate. The negotiations had already lasted too long, and we were wrestling over small policy details: this time, it was how the burden of reducing 0.2 megatons of carbon dioxide emissions would be shared. Again, many of the compromises I suggested favored the Greens, but as usual they thought that we weren't defending their interests enough. No one wanted to budge.

After spending days discussing this with the five leaders before the official budget negotiations even began, I got so frustrated that I decided to let the two leaders handle their conflict on their own. I told Maria Ohisalo, the leader of the Greens, and Annika Saarikko, leader of the Center Party, that I had done all I could and I would accept any decision they came to.

Leaving the room was not just a tactic to preserve my sanity—it was also a strategic move. Without the SDP, the two parties were simply at loggerheads. After spending even more time alone together in the room, they were forced to admit they needed us to mediate because they couldn't make any decisions without us.

When I returned to the table the next morning, I asked them what they'd decided. The mood was completely different: the Greens were humble and conciliatory toward me. They had realized that they didn't have any leverage without us in the room because the Center Party is known for their ability to get tough if necessary. The Center Party was surprised that the Greens had totally lost their confidence after realizing what they were up against. The ultimate solution was almost the same as the previous drafts that I'd presented to the parties, with a few extra wins for the Center Party.

However frustrated I felt behind closed doors by the endless negotiations involved in a coalition government, I always tried to keep my cool outside. At the end of the negotiations, I praised the other leaders on their ability to find solutions on difficult issues, and moved on to the next task.

○

There have only been a few occasions when I have been seriously angry with some of my coalition partners—not just a bit frustrated, but angry. And on one of those occasions I almost turned in my resignation and dismantled the government.

At the beginning of every term, the government negotiates and agrees on a plan, called a "frame," for how much money it will spend over the next four years. This framework isn't legally binding, but it has been customary for governments to commit to these frameworks in their programs and not exceed them for political purposes, to avoid sudden extra spending. Problems arise because the frame restricts only spending and excludes taxation, which limits the government's flexibility to make significant policy changes. So the frames aren't a tool for balancing state finances, but rather for keeping the government close to its proposed spending limits throughout the term. These frames have nothing to do with what is happening outside in the real world—whether we are in a recession, or if the economy is growing, doesn't matter. But for some people, staying within these frames is an almost sacred thing. In Finland, the "official truth" has been that those who question the frame system, or go against it, are reckless in handling the state's finances.

Of course, this conventional wisdom has been weaponized most frequently by right-wing parties that want to restrain, and in many cases cut, public spending and don't want to use taxation as a tool to balance our budget. Meanwhile, the Social Democrats have criticized the system as imbalanced because it only evaluates spending, not financing, and so is detached from the real economy. And as you may remember, the Center Party is often caught in the middle between the right and the left. They always struggled with their role in our government, torn between making concessions to the center-left government and appealing to the right-wing conservative opposition in hopes of gaining seats in the next elections.

Every spring, the government holds a session on spending limits in which it evaluates and updates the framework. Because of the pandemic and its serious economic consequences, our government had to set unprecedented extra budgets and exceed the framework and spending limits that we'd agreed on at the beginning of our term. These measures weren't opposed by the right-wing parties, quite the contrary—many times, they demanded even more support, for different purposes. But one of the things you can do as the opposition is to be inconsistent, so when it was time for overall evaluations of spending, they would criticize the government for loose economic policies and the fact that we, like every country, had to take on more debt to cope with COVID. For most of the parties in government, these accusations from the opposition weren't an issue, but for the Center Party the criticism hit harder.

If we had decided to stay within the original spending frame, it would have meant huge cuts to public spending, which would have been a social and economic catastrophe in the middle of an ongoing global crisis. Still, in spring 2021, the Center Party, which led the Ministry of Finance, wanted to return to these limits. For the SDP and other parties in the government, this was unacceptable. And so the routine government session on spending limits, which should have lasted no more than a few days, transformed into nine days of negotiations that almost brought down the government.

The parties had negotiated well beforehand and agreed on the majority of measures that we would be discussing in the midterm session. So when the Center Party entered the session with radical and unrealistic demands, it was obvious that public spending and fiscal balance were not their only worries. I still think today that what they really wanted was to leave the government, which had always been an ambivalent enterprise for them, but they didn't want to take the blame for it in the middle of a global crisis. In their ideal scenario, I assume, the right-wing National Coalition Party could have joined the government in their place, and they would have had enough time to raise their support as members of the opposition before elections in 2023. So they orchestrated a situation in which the midterm session would descend into crisis. What they didn't anticipate was how I would handle it—staying extremely calm and patient, and refusing to escalate despite their many attempts.

I made a plan. The Center Party was trying to ignite a scandal in the press, so I needed to win the public debate. I would stay composed and, meanwhile, gather support for the SDP's narrative from all the other parties both behind closed doors and out in the public. My team and I started systematically explaining to the press what was happening, shooting down false accusations and information. At the negotiating table, my team and I would dominate the discussion with information, and we wouldn't be provoked. I also needed to make sure the negotiations moved forward steadily, reaching compromises on every decision that came to the table. Ensuring support from the other three parties was essential, so we kept them well informed.

Soon, the Center Party had lost both the public debate and the discussions in the negotiations four to one. They still had the power to resist compromise, but it became clear to everyone that if they continued their policy of obstinacy, it would be their fault if the government collapsed, which would hurt their chances in the elections that would follow. This pressure meant they finally began to negotiate with purpose, and we began to make some progress.

Finally, when almost everything about the framework was settled,

I met with the leader of the Center Party, Annika Saarikko, to go through the compromise. I anticipated some last-minute demands—it was their custom—but after so many days of infuriating behavior, I had no patience for any additional requests.

Saarikko proposed employment measures to strengthen public finances by 200 million euros. In practice, it would have meant cuts to unemployment benefits. I stood up and raised my voice: I wouldn't approve any new demands from them. I left the room, slamming the door behind me. For me, it was simply out of the question to cut social benefits in the middle of COVID, but on top of that issue, Saarikko had hinted that the Center Party might cause problems in parliament when the European MMF agreement—which, remember, required a two-thirds majority—came to a vote. After explaining the situation to the other party leaders, I returned to the prime minister's residence and called an emergency meeting with the SDP minister group. I told them that I was ready to dissolve the government and initiate new elections if the Center Party didn't drop their newest claim. These weren't empty words.

One of the reasons these negotiations had been so difficult was that some of our own people had been meddling in the talks on the side, thinking that they were being clever by gathering information. The interference had only prolonged the process; gossip has a way of leaving communication in tangles. However, because I knew people had been gossiping about the negotiations, I was able to use this to my advantage: I knew our people would contact their counterparts from the Center Party to say that I was dead serious and their plan would end badly if they didn't back down. Soon enough, I got a text message from Saarikko saying she was ready to agree on what had previously been negotiated.

I developed a lot of patience handling these situations. But after the Center Party tried to entrap me, my patience was gone. I didn't answer Saarikko's text immediately, but decided to wait until I got back to the House of Estates, where we held the meetings.

It is usually very satisfying to conclude negotiations and find solutions to difficult problems. This time I wasn't relieved—I was just fed up with the political circus. Even though the government survived, the ordeal harmed the relationship between us and the Center Party. They gained almost nothing from their scheme, but they lost influence within the government, and their image took a hit publicly, too. Just as negotiators should always be two steps ahead, anyone attempting the risky move of creating drama for leverage should, too. Always have an exit strategy.

The political lesson is: you shouldn't create a crisis if you don't know how to walk out of it.

# 10.

# SCANDALS

**Politicians working at a high level** will have to deal with scandals and turbulence at some point in their career. It is inevitable today, when social media platforms and the twenty-four-hour news cycle reward extreme and polarizing stories to generate clicks and advertising revenue; of course, private people might easily find themselves the center of a social media firestorm for different reasons. Sometimes these scandals are the result of one's actions, political or personal, but other times they can appear almost out of nowhere and take unpredictable forms. These are in many ways harder to handle, as the scandals or their magnitude don't make much sense.

The most serious political scandals are related to misuse of power, status, or public funding, or corruption or other criminal activities. These are unfortunately not uncommon when we look at the world. The scandals that I had to deal with were different—they related to my personal life and questions about my morality, and were, in many cases, laced with sexism and double standards. I can say without a doubt that I have firsthand experience of how media scandals appear and what kind of twists and turns they can take.

Beyond an initial salacious story or detail, scandals often take turns that are totally unexpected: throughout the media cycle, which always lasted much longer than I would have expected, new pieces of information emerge just when you think it is over. Designed to prolong the prurience, this information could be something done by others, without your knowledge or ability to control. How to respond is complicated. So many times, I've heard some media expert or consultant offer naive comments to the press, advising anyone suffering through a scandal just to explain everything and apologize. But it is impossible to explain everything when you can't even know what everything might be, and it is insane to apologize when the accusations might be irrational, or nobody really knows what "crime" or offense was committed.

Scandals can't just be stopped once the press smells a selling story and every newspaper and journalist wants to put their own spin on it. When this is happening, it can be deeply exhausting, and it can last for a long time. Resignation—emotionally or literally, from your job—can start to sound appealing, even if the inciting incident itself was never that serious.

In my own experience, the only thing you can do is to wait until the first wave of turmoil has passed; trying to intervene before that is like shouting into a high wind. After this, you can start dealing with the situation, correcting misinformation and storylines, and working your way out. I have always stepped in front of cameras to answer any questions the press might have; this means I have answered such absurd questions during my career that it has felt like my brain was melting. But I've always done so in a calm and patient manner. That is the only way to show people that there is nothing to hide—and that there was never that much to report in the first place, even if the headlines were the size of a building.

Nevertheless, it is extremely consuming to be at the center of media turbulence and scrutiny. Different people cope with these situations differently. Some can handle a lot, compartmentalize, and continue working; others are traumatized following public exposure. But I think that everyone who deals with extensive media scrutiny feels hurt and vulnerable at some point, and I am no exception. On top of the emotional burdens, it took a lot of time and energy, not only from me but from my entire team, to deal with these situations. It was incredibly frustrating to be sidetracked from the actual work that I wanted and needed to focus on. And there was never a break until the scandal eventually died out.

I went into the prime minister job believing I had a good under-standing of the media. While I knew the attention, and pressure, would increase once I took the office, I thought that attention would center on my work and my politics. I anticipated that people would try to take me down, which happens with any politician at a high level. But I assumed that these attacks would take a familiar form: criticism of my policies and my abilities. Maybe, if I was unlucky or made a major mistake, there would be debates over whether I had adhered to the prime minister's mandate.

I was wrong. What wouldn't have merited more than a mention in the news for many other leaders would balloon into weeks of stories dissecting my appearance, my behavior, and my suitability for public office. There were so many of these incidents that my team and I now simply refer to them as "the scandals." You might have even heard about some of them.

## 1. The Blazer Scandal

My term as prime minister began with a slew of political crises, and the huge attention from the press, both in Finland and internationally, only added to the responsibilities I faced as soon as I took office. My team did a great job balancing the endless media requests with everything else that was on my plate. While political work took priority, it was still important to systematically go through these requests and respond to them. I wanted to tell the public about the work our government was doing.

One of my goals was to model a different, more modern way of being a politician that would make a political career seem more accessible to young people, especially women. For me it was very important to be myself and not change to fit some stereotype of a prime minister. So when the Finnish fashion magazine *Trendi* requested an interview with me some months after I started my term, we decided it would be a good opportunity to reach a female audience to tell them about our government's policies. The magazine wanted to put me on the cover and publish the interview accompanied by a photo spread, and we arranged the shoot so that it would take as little time as possible away from whatever political situation I'd be dealing with at the time.

I do not believe fashion is frivolous, but I don't think about it very much, and especially didn't when I was in office. I tried to choose plain, usually black, professional clothes that were appropriate to the setting and wouldn't distract from whatever I was saying or doing. Of course, when you appear on the cover of a magazine, the clothes you wear will be more striking than what you might wear to an eight-hour budget negotiation. And when you're being featured in a magazine, a professional stylist will be the one choosing your wardrobe. All of this is standard, and it wasn't as if a female politician had never been on the cover of a magazine before.

When I showed up to the *Trendi* shoot, the magazine team was well prepared because they knew I had very little time—they had a clear vision for the photo spread. Finland has a strong tradition of jewelry design. During the twentieth century, many jewelry workshops sprang up across the country, and designers developed a distinctive Nordic look that combined organic forms of modernism with a futuristic touch. (The Finnish designer Björn Weckström made the necklace that Carrie Fisher wears in the final scene of the first *Star Wars* film.) During this magazine shoot, the stylist wanted to gesture toward this national history by highlighting the necklace I would be wearing, which was a vintage design by Kalevala Koru. The editors asked if I minded wearing a suit jacket, which had also been made by a Finnish brand, without a shirt underneath so that the necklace would be the focal point of the shot.

I didn't see a problem with it. The outfit didn't feel or look scandalous, and there was nothing risqué showing. I wanted to take the photos and move on with my day. I think the entire shoot took less than half an hour, and I left for whatever was next on the schedule.

When the article was published about a month later, however, it caused a huge public debate. Some people thought the photos were too provocative and inappropriate for a politician; others thought this reaction was misogynist and outdated. It was like a tennis match: when someone asked whether it was appropriate for a prime minister to dress this way, someone else would celebrate the appearance of a confident young woman on the international political stage. "If you had to generalize it," the editor in chief of *Trendi* said, "it will be men saying it was wrong, and women saying it was fabulous." Soon people—of all genders—were taking photos of themselves wearing blazers without tops underneath and posting them to Instagram with the hashtag #imwithsanna.

Like many media frenzies, this began on social media platforms and hit the headlines when tabloids saw an interesting story. What started as a small, though harsh and sexist, discourse on social media became a symbolic clash between conservative and liberal values. For me, the debate felt totally out of proportion; everything I said in the interview was left behind and the entire focus was on my appearance and even made it into the international press. Media experts of all persuasions and interests were asked to analyze what I meant to communicate through the photos. The reality was that I wanted and tried to communicate with my words and thoughts in the actual interview and didn't focus on the photo shoot at all.

Since the article was published, papers have done countless stories and headlines about my appearance: the height of my heels or the size of my jewelry, the cost of my clothing or just endless articles about how my style has allegedly "changed." The same is true for so many women in the public eye. Many times these stories have moralistic or even sexualized attitudes: it's a typical strategy for putting women "in their place." Focusing on looks, rather than substance, and then claiming that this is exactly what women themselves want is a way to trap us. In politics, business, culture, and many other areas, people usually want to be recognized for what they do or say, and not for how they look, unless their work is based on appearances. More broadly, we shouldn't view the female face and body as subjects for judgment—and certainly not as subjects of discussion or argument. I have always admired people who have the courage to be themselves, even if it opens them up to criticism. As the scandals proliferated, I realized that it was important for me to model this approach to life as well.

## 2. The Breakfast Scandal

I had my hands full with work as new waves of COVID emerged and we were balancing restrictions with the desire to keep society as open as possible. It wasn't until late spring 2021 that the pandemic really began to calm down. Temperatures outside rose, sunlight increased, and society opened up again after a period of hibernation that had gone on much longer than usual.

At the beginning of COVID, my family and I had moved into the prime minister's residence, Kesäranta, an old wooden villa by the sea in Helsinki. Compared to analogous residences in other countries, Kesäranta is unpretentious, but the building and location are beautiful, and my daughter loved living there. It has a big yard to play in.

The building is also used for government meetings and events for international guests. My family and I were living upstairs, in the private residence, but most of the entertaining and meetings happened on the ground floor, and during COVID the basement was transformed into a remote meeting room to participate in EU and international affairs. Two of my favorite places were the upstairs balcony overlooking the sea, where I enjoyed my morning coffee in the summertime, and the wooden sauna, which was the only place I could really relax when handling the pandemic. Sauna is an important cultural aspect of Finnish life; the word *sauna* is Finnish, and the type of sauna used in most Western countries is our invention. Our winters are cold and dark, and the sauna is the place where we Finns go—by ourselves or with our families and friends—to be warm and relax. I used to go there after a long workday, once Emma had gone to sleep, and I would listen to music and think in peace.

I got a tour of the house after I started the job in January 2020: a public official took me through the house rules, the staff who worked there, and what kinds of things you are entitled to as part of living there as prime minister. The government document that contained all these rules and guidelines was created before my time, and it was updated by senior government officials before I took office. In addition to rules explaining how the facilities could be used for private events and the introductions to cleaners, gardeners, and the rest of the house staff, I was told that while living in Kesäranta my family and I were entitled to some groceries and meals—including breakfast. I was surprised by this, but as I got used to the job, it made more sense to me. It was incredibly useful, especially later during COVID, when our family was trying to avoid outside contacts and I was working around the clock.

I never thought to question this long-standing protocol, and other prime ministers had used the same services with no complaints. Then, in the spring of 2021, a journalist asked to see the receipts for purchases made by the house staff of Kesäranta. The public officials who were in charge declined on the grounds that the receipts contained private information about our family—diets and so on—that it is not legal to make publicly available. Security officials also wanted to make sure that the store where the groceries were purchased wasn't disclosed, for safety reasons.

But the government officials' refusal to turn over these receipts aroused suspicions. Questions from the media began to pile up. *We can't see the receipts, so we don't know what she's using taxpayer money to buy. What if she was using the funds to buy personal items, and not only groceries?*

Then things got even more personal. After sixteen years together, Markus and I had our small wedding at Kesäranta in August 2020. We paid for everything ourselves, and we kept all our receipts. But some journalists began to demand proof that I had not used taxpayer money to celebrate my marriage. One paper even threatened to publish a piece suggesting my wedding was paid for by public money if I didn't hand over my personal receipts. I declined as it was an intrusive, outrageous demand, and in the end the story was never published.

Although I hadn't done anything different than my predecessors— I had followed all the guidelines—the questions continued and comments shifted into moral territory. *Is Sanna Marin so greedy, so stingy, that she can't buy her own milk? She already gets paid so much!*

Naturally, as the media scandal persisted it took different angles. By now it was sometimes referred to as "breakfastgate." The focus shifted to whether the benefits were legal at all, and, if so, how they should be taxed. Before this the public officials involved, many of them trained lawyers, had systematically interpreted the legislation in a way that these costs were included as a part of living in Kesäranta, just like maintenance and other services of the residence.

At this point, I'd already said that I would pay back the full cost of the groceries that totaled approximately 850 euros per month, so about 15,000 euros from the previous year and a half. Municipal elections were approaching, and I wanted the storm to die down so that I could talk about something in the debates besides my family's yogurt habits. I was of course in favor of clarifying the situation, because I had done nothing out of the ordinary and taxation is an extremely serious matter in Finland, so I asked public officials to collaborate with the taxation authorities to determine how the policy should be taxed.

For me and my team it was crucially important to stop the scandal from spreading, and the only way to do this was to have an official explanation about what was going on. Getting to the bottom of the situation and gathering all the information was difficult and slow, and when we couldn't provide answers immediately, new questions flooded in. I felt helpless. Over the course of the events, we learned that the public officials who gave me instructions had ended up being wrong about taxation. So a preliminary inquiry was made by the police; the public officials who had written the original document containing all the house guidelines were questioned after the Office of the Chancellor of Justice determined that their interpretation of the legislation had been incorrect. I wasn't personally investigated because I had no reason not to trust the information given to me.

The storylines increased in the media and "breakfastgate" took a turn every time there was something new, usually small, to cover.

It lasted all the way up to the elections. Then, the story just died. Nobody was interested anymore.

Through this case, I learned the hard way what it means to be in the middle of intense media scrutiny. Media news cycles are relentless and sometimes the pace collides with the fact that all details are not available right away. This experience also taught me that when the media is putting their focus more and more on chasing clicks, the sense of proportion gets easily lost. Don't get me wrong, I respect the media and their work greatly. We need free and objective media for our democracy to work and thrive. And eventually, they did reveal an error in the official instructions, which was of course a good thing. But still to this day I can't quite comprehend the immense scale of the stories. There were even hints that I should be thinking about resigning because of this.

One very crucial thing to remember in these kinds of situations is that there is really no room for incorrect information. When you make a statement, you should be totally sure of the facts. But of course, life is not that simple. Life is messy and unmanageable. Sometimes it is just wiser to accept that you can't control everything. You just have to keep your cool and push forward. And despite how bad you feel, you have to remember that eventually all storms pass, new media frenzies fill the space, and when time goes on, things might even sometimes fall into perspective.

Although it may have looked like I had weathered the scandal well, and my support remained high throughout that period, I have to admit that I felt beaten down. I deeply appreciated the support and sympathy I received at the time from citizens; it helped my morale to be reminded that others could see that the scrutiny was disproportionate. And I would need the lessons I learned as my term went on.

## 3. The phone scandal

In December 2021, after almost two years of dealing with the COVID crisis, Finland had been able to steadily ease many restrictions and open our society with the help of vaccinations and the digital COVID pass. Safety protocols were still in place, but it was possible to gather with other people and go out to restaurants and even some events. Things had also settled down to the point that I had the opportunity to take a full weekend off, and I intended to spend it with my husband. I think many can relate; it's very difficult to find quality time with your partner when you work and have a small child. The prime minister's schedule makes things even more difficult. While Markus was always understanding and supportive, we were both very much looking forward to getting the chance to spend a day doing normal things that couples do on their days off. We decided not to stay at Kesäranta but in the apartment near parliament that I still owned, and my mother agreed to take care of Emma. We planned to do some shopping, followed by dinner at a restaurant with a few friends—the kind of day you take for granted when you can do it anytime.

Markus and I were on our way to the restaurant when I got a phone call from my state secretary. When I was prime minister, I had three work phones: a parliamentary phone, which was my primary phone that I used for daily contact and apps; a minister phone, which didn't have any social media apps or other security vulnerabilities, which I used for international contacts and official matters as prime minister; and a third phone that I didn't personally carry but was arranged for me to use when I had to deal with high-security issues. In general, I carried the first two with me during workdays, but I had left my minister phone at home that night on purpose. All my necessary contacts were on the parliamentary phone, and my advisors knew how to reach me. I also had security officers with me who would alert me to any emergencies. My state secretary called me on my parliamentary phone and explained that our foreign minister might have COVID.

At that time, Finland's general COVID guidelines written by health authorities advised people who had received two vaccinations to continue their lives as usual if they found they were exposed to COVID; self-isolation was no longer recommended.

As a result, my state secretary instructed me to continue as normal; the guidelines meant the situation wouldn't affect me or other ministers at that point. He said he would contact me if things changed and I didn't question his advice. I knew the protocol well, I'd had two vaccinations already, and I hadn't been in that close contact with the foreign minister and not in a time frame that would have made me contagious to others in the worst-case scenario.

Markus and I went to the restaurant, met our friends, had dinner, and then went to a small cocktail bar. After that, the group of us went to a club. Nothing significant happened, either at the club or on my phone—my state secretary didn't get back to me, and my security didn't receive any messages or calls about the situation. It was nice to be out with our friends. Markus and I went back to the apartment and went to sleep, happy to have finally gotten to enjoy a day and evening together.

I woke up early the next day and looked at my two phones, as I did every morning. On my minister phone, I saw the routine text the cabinet received every day: a daily dispatch with news and information about the COVID situation and other topics that might require frequent updates. It wasn't a text meant specifically for me—every minister and their cabinets, as well as many other staff and officials, received it. But it did contain different, more cautious instructions than what I had received the night before. These were also different from the guidelines the public had been advised to follow by health officials. The message instructed anyone who had been in the same room with the foreign minister on Friday to self-isolate, just in case.

I called my state secretary to ask what it meant—why should we isolate against general instructions, and why hadn't I been informed about this the night before? As a precaution, I took a home COVID test immediately—negative—and then took another official test later that day, also negative. But I was on high alert. I knew this wouldn't stop the press going after me. I had been out the previous night and against an instruction that was exceptionally sent in a daily dispatch text to many people.

That evening, on a Sunday, videos and photos of me at the bar began to appear on news websites. It wasn't anything dramatic or scandalous—no wild dancing—just reports that I was there. But journalists soon put two and two together, and they began to ask why I had been at a bar when I should have been home isolating because our minister had COVID.

I discussed the situation with Krista Kiuru, the minister who was one of the key players in charge of handling COVID, and she was surprised that the ministers had received sudden instructions that contradicted what we had told the public. These stricter instructions were released by public officials from the prime minister's office that was in charge of general safety protocol. Even I hadn't heard about these instructions earlier. For her the main concern was how could we justify telling doctors, nurses, and social workers to go to work having been exposed to COVID when government officials had to follow stricter, more careful instructions.

On Sunday evening we immediately started to answer all the media's questions—and face the inevitable criticism from the opposition. As I didn't have COVID and hadn't exposed anyone, the discussion couldn't linger on the public health threat. But there was energy in the story, and the press was loath to let that go to waste. So the questions began to center on the fact that I hadn't received the stricter instructions the night I'd been out with my friends—why didn't I have the minister phone with me? I explained truthfully that I'd left the phone at home on purpose; I didn't need it on my night out, I didn't intend to contact my foreign colleagues from a cocktail bar, and I was reachable by my parliamentary phone that I use as a primary phone every day. There were also security officers with me the entire time, so the idea that I wouldn't get the information I needed to do my job in case of an emergency was ludicrous.

Nevertheless, because there were multiple possible avenues to criticize my behavior, the scandal evolved and grew. Neither question—why didn't I isolate, and why didn't I have both phones with me—had an interesting answer. But because the situation was extremely embarrassing to me as a leader who had handled COVID well so far, the press pushed the story as if it were an actual catastrophe. I was also embarrassed I hadn't known about the new instructions, which had been written about a week earlier. They were only available on a government intranet page, not circulated among the government staff, which was unusual. As the prime minister, I received information in briefings collated for me, but none of my advisors, or my secretary, had noticed or was personally told about the new guidelines.

The situation was tricky because there were two questions about my behavior rather than just one, and the press could keep publishing articles suggesting that I must be hiding something. And beneath these questions was the perennial issue people liked to bring up when it came to my appearance or behavior: Was it really appropriate for a leader to be doing something so normal as going to a bar with her friends?

As it became obvious the story wasn't going to settle, we held a large press conference in the courtyard of the parliament building on that Tuesday. I always preferred to meet the media in an open setting in order to highlight that I had nothing to hide, and I answered questions as long as it took to get through them. Many of the media's questions were valid, and they helped me clarify the situation quickly. Others, however, were designed to prolong the drama.

"Why did you drink Corona beer?" one journalist from a tabloid asked. "Was that a joke, or just a coincidence?" As if I had been trying to make some kind of statement with the beer I drank.

In Finland, we refer to Covid as "Korona." Although it's not spelled the same, it does sound like the Mexican beer. I had to hold back my amusement—and also frustration at the absurdity of where the conversation was going. It was important to stay reasonable so that I couldn't be portrayed as volatile, or have my words twisted.

"I drank beer," I said. I couldn't remember the specific beer I drank. I drank whatever beer they had in the bar. It wasn't something I put any thought into. It wasn't a statement, and I still don't quite understand what the statement would have been if I had been trying to make one.

In the end the media lost interest in the story, and I think it was a combination of two factors. First, I showed up to answer all the questions and took responsibility—as the situation was very difficult for me, I had no other choice but to apologize for not knowing about the new instructions and acting accordingly; and as nothing actually happened, there wasn't much to continue with. The second reason was that the press found out that two male ministers from the Center Party had also missed information about the guidance and had been out attending events of their own. Suddenly it wasn't just me who was immoral or liable—we could point to a wider problem in the information flow. Nevertheless, one journalist did ask me if it felt like I was the only person being pressured about the situation, given that the other ministers didn't have to hold press conferences or answer silly questions. I replied simply that I took responsibility for my own actions.

As I'd learned by then, with both political and personal scandals, transparency is the best tactic. I always felt that if I showed up in front of the press and answered questions straightforwardly and honestly—even the silly ones—it would help me deal with the situation and let me get back to work. More or less, this was the case. But not always . . .

## 4. The Dancing Scandal

By the time the summer of 2022 arrived, my team and I had an understanding of how the scandal cycle worked. A scoop or story gets things rolling, but once the facts are checked and the initial excitement might be revealed to be premature, the story doesn't just go away. Often, the media, eager to maintain the momentum of a provocative narrative, finds a way to keep it going into a new phase. This new phase is impossible to predict; it will involve links to people and events and ideas that would have never occurred to us before journalists began covering them. Once the scandal reaches this second phase, it becomes a huge, tangled mess that is very difficult to control.

At the end of that summer, I had a weekend off when many people in Finland were still on their own vacations. I decided to spend an evening with friends. One of my best friends, Ilmari Nurminen, a member of parliament, and his boyfriend invited me and a few others over to spend a warm summer evening on their rooftop terrace, drinking wine and just having a fun time.

We were listening to music, dancing, and singing, as often happens when gay men and women get together. Someone put on the song "The Beast Is Released" by the famous Finnish pop singer Antti Tuisku, and we started dancing. We hadn't had very much to drink, but like many people of our generation, we filmed ourselves dancing and lip-syncing along—in an exaggerated, outrageous way, as a joke—because we really loved the song. It has silly lyrics and a good beat. The story isn't exactly complicated, or unheard of. After enjoying a few hours at their place, we headed off to see some other friends at a female couple's apartment. For me, it was a very fun, and very comfortable environment; I was raised in a rainbow family, so I have spent most of my life as part of a liberal, queer community where everyone is accepted for who they are. Again, we chatted, sang, and danced—what people do at parties.

One of the guests there maintained a small private Instagram account. I had known her for some time, and I didn't mind her sharing some stories of the group of us dancing. Like all Instagram stories, the video would only be visible for twenty-four hours. The account was private, so it shouldn't have been possible to publish any of the material publicly without her consent. We danced, sang, and laughed so much, and for me it was one of the most joyous nights that summer. We met up with more friends at a bar and went to a club, and then I went home with my security, who had been in range the entire night.

Besides being an especially good time, it was an uneventful evening—just a fun night out with friends, nothing I'd otherwise consider special, except for the fact that it happened so rarely for a prime minister. It had been a long time since I'd had a proper summer holiday like this, and I was ready to return to work and lead our party into the next parliamentary elections, which would be held the following April.

The evening wouldn't become significant for about two weeks—not until the SDP's annual parliamentary group summer meeting in August. Every year, the entire group, which at that time was around forty parliamentarians plus other staff, travels to some part of Finland to meet citizens, hold official meetings, and connect with each other and with the media. The summer meeting is widely regarded as a key occasion where representatives from major media outlets gather alongside political figures for shared events and an evening dinner—a chance for off-the-record conversations and insights ahead of the political season's autumn kickoff. And, as we were the PM party in power, our presence ensured a full house.

That year, we went to Kuopio, a city with just over 120,000 residents in the eastern part of Finland. The first day of the meeting was coming to a close, and at dinner, I was seated next to some representatives of the city. I was chatting with them about the lovely visit that I had made to one of their elementary schools that morning when, suddenly, my special advisor for media and communications, Iida Vallin, appeared at my side. Her face was pale.

"Sanna," she whispered, "you have to come outside now."

"What is it?" I whispered back. "Can't it wait until after dinner?"

I could see the answer on her face. "Sanna," she repeated, "you have to come out now."

In the hallway she elaborated, though not much. "There is footage circulating," she said.

You probably know the footage she was talking about. She held out her phone to me: I was dancing in a provocative manner, wearing a black top and white jeans, singing along to "The Beast Is Released" at my friend's apartment. As soon as she showed it to me, I realized immediately what would happen, the sequence of events. It would cause a terrible uproar. An initial round of political accusations and condemnations would die down, and in their absence a new phase of scandal, rooted in morality, would grow. Discussion would continue for weeks. It was going to be awful.

Still, I stayed calm. My reflex, a self-protective mechanism, was to switch off my emotions, and I immediately began to prepare. I knew I could not change that situation—it was the reality now. So we would have to simply handle it. Even though nothing with concrete political consequences had happened, it would be a nightmare to have to answer to the media and to explain the videos.

By this point, the footage hadn't yet hit the news—a friend of Iida's, who was the special advisor to Minister Kiuru, had seen it circulating in a private political WhatsApp group. The press had the footage, but it hadn't yet been published. The video had been taken from the private Instagram account; someone must have leaked it from there, but I had no idea who. In Finland, publishing images or recordings taken in private homes or on private property is generally not permitted, so journalists couldn't necessarily publish it on a newspaper's website. But if the footage was widely shared already, it could be considered public knowledge, and the press could publish it. And the person behind the leak had made sure this would happen.

In other words, we were waiting for it to go public, and we were surrounded by journalists.

Ilmari, the friend who'd hosted the gathering, was at the meeting with us. I pulled him from the dinner and showed him the footage. His reaction was not exactly calm; he was terrified. Iida was furious at him, though of course it wasn't his fault. We went to find Antti Lindtman, the leader of the parliamentary group, and Tuulia Pitkänen, my chief of staff, and the four of us—Iida, Tuulia, Antti, and I—snuck out of the restaurant and into one of the big vans that the prime minister's office uses for transportation. It was the least obvious place we could think of, though in retrospect it does sound like something out of a movie. The fact that the press was just a few dozen meters away, unaware of the scandal that was about to break, didn't help the situation.

We began to go through what we thought would happen: How big of a deal it would be? What would the media focus on first? What should our immediate response be?

While we were in the van, the story broke in at least one outlet. We saw it on our phones, and then, outside, though the van's tinted windows were dark, we could see the journalists walking around in the yard in front of the restaurant, making calls. We could see from their body language that they were getting increasingly excited.

The scene that unfolded was truly absurd: we became very quiet as we watched the journalists talking to each other and on their phones, unaware that we were sitting right in front of them. We were also acutely aware that we were trapped in the van. If any of us got out, we'd be photographed emerging from an emergency van meeting upon the breaking news of a major media scandal.

Finally, after about fifteen or twenty minutes, the journalists went back inside. We looked around, saw the coast was clear, and left the van separately. Iida and I went back to the venue to continue hosting as if nothing were happening; the van then drove around the corner so Antti and Tuulia could walk back in together without arousing suspicions. We'd be dealing with this all night, and for much longer.

The situation was new to everyone, and it wasn't exactly a political scandal on par with misuse of power. Although we were all in the unique situation of being relatively isolated in the same place with each other, the media didn't react with the force it would develop later. These dinners were informal, and no one was running around trying to get comments from me. At first it looked like the journalists didn't even think it was that big of a deal. Someone from my team stayed at the venue to observe the media's reactions; they ended up going to a bar after dinner. Meanwhile, Tuulia, Iida, and I went to my hotel room to strategize until 2 a.m. What political felony would they accuse me of? It was clear from the beginning that there had been no real wrongdoing. Obviously, dancing in an apartment and having someone post videos of that on a private Instagram account breaks no law, leaves no duty unattended, hurts no one, and does not qualify as being dishonest. But we knew that didn't matter. And because it didn't matter, it would be much harder to put out the fire. The discussion could take any form the press might come up with.

The next morning, Iida's phone was overloaded with calls and messages. The press, many of whom had spent a wild night out in Kuopio, needed a comment from the prime minister.

I woke up early, drank an oat latte, and put on a plain white T-shirt, wanting to look as neutral as possible. We were holding a press conference in the foyer of the Kuopio music hall. The session didn't last that long, about ten minutes, but answering those initial questions felt like an eternity. *What happened? Is this footage real? Were intoxticating substances used?*

*How much alcohol did you drink?* I haven't calculated the amount.

*Did you try to distract your security?* No, my security was near the apartment and me the entire evening. (I did have my two phones with me—I wouldn't make that mistake again.)

*Who filmed these videos? Where? When? Are there more? Are you being hacked? Are you being blackmailed?*

*Is this part of your strategy to shake the prime minister institution?* No. I feel bad that these videos have leaked.

*Who leaked the videos?* I don't know who leaked the videos. (I don't believe the one who posted them leaked them to the press.)

*It feels bad for me to ask these questions,* one journalist began. *Currently people are discussing that "flour" is slang that means amphetamine or cocaine in Helsinki. Why is someone in the video saying "flour"?*

Of course, the questions around drugs were the most serious. The same night the video was released, commenters on an anonymous internet forum with a lot of far-right and misogynist content began to claim that I was clearly on drugs in the videos. Someone took a screenshot from the video, upped the saturation, and Photoshopped reflections from an iPhone on the table to look like lines of white powder. Someone else argued that there wasn't enough alcohol visible in the videos, so we must have been doing drugs instead. (My response to that is that this party was made up of girls and gays—we know how to have fun without getting completely drunk.) Some commenter on a forum suggested that one of the women in the video wasn't actually singing along to the lyrics of the song, but saying something else: "flour gang." No one knows what she was saying, and in fact, "flour" isn't slang for anything in Helsinki—not drugs or anything else to my knowledge. The journalist was making that up, or relying on the wishful thinking that was proliferating on internet forums.

I for sure didn't use drugs, and I didn't see anyone else use drugs, either—in fact, I had never really seen anyone do drugs. When I was younger I was interested in party politics, not partying; I was a serious, driven person and felt I didn't have time to spend at the bar every weekend. That's how I became the prime minister!

Still, the night before, we had noticed that some of these far-right platforms were hinting that there had been drugs at the party. So when I prepared for these questions, I decided I was going to say truthfully that I had never done drugs, and furthermore that I had never even seen anyone do drugs in my life.

Then, in the middle of the night, I woke up suddenly and sat up in my hotel bed. *Oh my God*, I thought, *oh no. I have seen somebody using cannabis—once, at a music festival in Italy. I didn't know them, but I did see them*. I was awake in the middle of the night worrying that I couldn't honestly say I'd never even seen someone do drugs. That's how bizarre the situation was.

Back to the press conference. *Why is someone in the video saying "flour"?* I didn't say flour, I don't know about this, I have no knowledge of drugs being at the party.

*Obviously the "flourgang" is using something?* I have danced, I have sung, I have partied, I have done fully legal things. (This became a meme.)

(Asking again.) *How did this footage leak?* I don't know.

*Are you going to change your behavior?* No, I'm going to be the same person that I have been so far, and I hope the public will accept that.

*Soon there will be elections, do Finnish people accept this kind of behavior from the prime minister?* People will have the right to decide for themselves.

The real political crime here, we realized, was that I didn't look or behave like a prime minister is expected to look or behave. I was too informal, too relaxed, and I danced in a way that was deemed promiscuous. I was at a party full of young people at someone's apartment instead of a staid dinner with eight courses and wine pairings. I was wearing a top and jeans instead of a pantsuit. I was hanging out with "influencers" (actually a group that consisted of politicians, dentists, human rights activists, and people from the culture sector and fashion industry) instead of "decent" people like businessmen. I was spending time off in a way that didn't tick the conservative box long reserved for heads of government. It was a perfect setup for a moral panic. And it didn't end after that press conference.

The contrast between the international media's cheerful, amused reaction to the story—look, Finland's liberal prime minister is so unconventional and fun! She likes to dance!—and the relentless criticism of the Finnish media was jarring. Around the world, politicians and public figures began to defend me—Hillary Clinton and Alexandria

Ocasio-Cortez filmed themselves dancing in support, and it was the subject of lighthearted bits on talk shows. "I know this is confusing to Americans so let me try to explain, some countries have leaders that don't have osteoporosis and they party," Trevor Noah joked. But the Finnish media would not let it go.

After my press conference, the Finnish press spent weeks searching for an angle that would force me to resign. One newspaper hired a sound expert (anonymous) to analyze the video to understand whether we used the word "flour." Naturally, the anonymous sound expert said there was no question—we did say it.

But the scandal didn't stay confined to traditional media—it spread into all areas of my life. We received information from security officials that WhatsApp groups were circulating a photo of a naked woman in a man's apartment, alleging it was me. The scam was elaborate; the images were of alleged text messages between a Finnish singer, who is a friend of mine, and another person, in which the singer says that the dark-haired woman in the picture is me. It wasn't difficult for the security experts to determine that the image originated on an adult website and had been used for different kinds of blackmail purposes around the world for years. Meanwhile, users on the forums responsible for spreading rumors of drug use had also encouraged people to try to hack the email and social media accounts of the people who'd been at the party, and we were getting worried calls from my friends, whose accounts were indeed being attacked. There were many more nasty things happening behind the scenes than were ever reported in the media. Because so many accusations and false narratives appeared at the same time on different forums and platforms, I suspected this was not only an organic scandal but also an orchestrated attack.

The initial scandal was based on an actual event—me dancing and spending a night out with friends—for which there was documentation, but it blew up because of doctored images and conspiracy theories hinting that there was something more to the story, like drugs or other illegal behavior. Dancing or drinking aren't scandalous enough to generate real political consequences. But creating a huge complicated web of narratives around a politician might be.

While the scam photos were quickly debunked, the media kept pushing: there had to be something they could get me for. The opposition leader of the right-wing Finns Party suggested that maybe the prime minister should take a drug test, just to clear up any suspicion. While some other parliamentarians had been saying something similar, the fact that a party leader would go on record with a newspaper gave the suggestion more weight. The press began asking why I wouldn't take a voluntary drug test.

I was furious that I was being pressured to undergo medical testing there was no basis or evidence for. How was it possible that I was being asked to take a drug test when no one had any proof of me doing drugs? Could anyone just falsely accuse me and require me to respond?

The answer is, apparently, yes, they can. The journalists began to hint that if I refused to take a drug test, I must have something to hide.

Since I hadn't done drugs and wanted the whole issue to be dealt with, I agreed to take a drug test.

The drug test was administered in Kesäranta by a healthcare professional according to official practices, on the Friday after the video leaked. We requested that they test for absolutely everything. We didn't want there to be any room for follow-up questions.

As soon as the test was over, my team and I began to suffer absurd, fleeting panics. What if there were poppy seeds in the bread I'd eaten that morning (remember that *Seinfeld* episode where Elaine takes a drug test and it comes back positive because of a poppy-seed muffin)? What if the tests showed a vague result for poppy seeds? Why hadn't we thought to ask the doctor if that was a risk? Had I even eaten poppy seeds that morning? The exhaustion of that absurd week was getting to me. Suddenly, we all began laughing—so hard that I had to sit on the floor. We had been working so much, nonstop, that we had become delirious. The whole thing was so ridiculous that at that moment it seemed the only fitting end to the saga would be that I would have to explain to the press that the drug test I'd taken had come back positive because of poppy seeds I couldn't remember eating. It was just so absurd. We were educated adults with real work to do. I was the prime minister! And I had spent days thinking about "The Beast Is Released" and whether people use the word "flour" to refer to cocaine!

We calmed down and got back to work the best we could. (The moment of levity was a relief, but I was still anxious about the whole situation.) Because we were preparing for the upcoming elections, our schedule was filled not only with governmental work but with political preparations as well. The next Monday, Tuulia and I were headed to the SDP office to a meeting with an advertising agency when the results came back: unsurprisingly, all negative.

The test results list was written in medical terminology—not street slang.

Suddenly Tuulia looked at me. "Why isn't Ecstasy mentioned?" she said. "Isn't that a party drug? Why isn't it being tested?"

"What?" I replied. "Why didn't they test for Ecstasy? Ecstasy is missing!"

"Wait. What is Ecstacy? Is it one of these?"

Immediately everyone grabbed their phone and began to type in "what is ecstasy."

Tuulia began texting with Iida, my communications advisor: if they didn't test for Ecstasy, it would look like we had something to hide. All of us knew that after a mistake like that, I would have no choice but to resign—that would be it.

Finally, after several minutes of frantic reading, Iida thought to call the doctor who administered the test. The doctor reassured her that Ecstasy was part of one of the substances on the list—they had definitely tested for it. It is an amphetamine derivative. At least we learned something that day.

Given the results of the drug test, we thought the scandal might finally die down. But then another wave came out of nowhere—and this one was actually very bad.

At the beginning of the following week, a new photo leaked. It wasn't from the same night at the apartment party—it was a photo from my own temporary home at Kesäranta.

It was once again a nice evening: some friends came over and went to the sauna, danced, swam, and drank some wine with food. But the photo that leaked from the night told a different story. It featured two women kissing in front of official Finnish government wallpaper. If that wasn't enough of a clue to where they were, one of the women held out a nameplate that read "FINLAND." I'd had no idea anyone had taken any photos like this, but since it was taken in the prime minister's residence, in front of official government wallpaper, I held myself responsible.

When this photo leaked, the mood was very, very grave. We didn't know if we would be able to survive it.

I had not apologized for the dancing videos, and I believed it was important not to apologize when I didn't have anything to apologize for. I believed, and still do believe, that it is important for politicians, and everyone, to be themselves and maintain private lives even when they're in office, as long as their duties don't suffer.

But I did apologize for that picture—not because two women were kissing but because the photo was taken in front of a formal government setting and as such could be interpreted as an insult to the institution. I should have been able to prevent this from happening.

We just couldn't believe it. No one had called for my resignation, and indeed most of my colleagues were incredibly supportive. But it was one of my worst weeks in office, and it wouldn't end.

Finally we decided that I had to give a speech and speak to people face to face. A week after the videos first leaked, our party held another summer meeting, this time for the ministerial group. Again, we always hold these conferences in different cities to allow the ministers to meet with people in different regions, and this time we were in Lahti, which is about the same size city as Kuopio but closer to Helsinki. We decided I should give the speech in the city square.

Hundreds of people gathered to see me speak that day. I'm sure some were there out of pure curiosity, but it seemed most had come in support. I rarely use notes or read from a paper when I give speeches in gatherings, and this was no exception. I just tried to speak from the heart, but my exhaustion was visible.

This was not a typical political speech analyzing the state of Europe and our government's policy, though I did begin with a more traditional discussion of political issues. Then, coming to the end of my speech, I addressed the dancing elephant in the room. "I believe that people look at the work that we actually do and not what we do in our private life. I am a human," I said with a trembling voice as tears rose to my eyes. People started applauding spontaneously. "And during these dark times I too need some joy, light, and fun. And that involves all sorts of photos and videos, which I would not like to see, and I know you would not like to see, but nonetheless are shown to us. It's private, it's joy, and it's life. But I haven't missed a single day of work or left a task undone."

The crowd was wildly supportive. After I left the podium, people of all ages came up to me to give me a hug and encouragement. Children said they'd skipped school because they wanted to come see me and take photos with me; older people assured me that they were on my side, too. Some elderly women were in tears, saying they felt I was treated so unfairly. The response was incredibly moving, and it drove home the divide between the press and the public. No one seemed to be outraged about what I'd done.

Finally it seemed like the scandal might actually die down, and it did after this. But not before a journalist approached Iida after the speech to ask a question: "Did she have to practice crying? Is this part of your strategy?"

○

Many times during my political career, my character and the way I genuinely am have been interpreted as some kind of provocation against the establishment. Just as often, my actions have been interpreted as a way of building an image. Countless times, journalists have asked me and my advisors why I did something or didn't do it—were my actions part of some media strategy they didn't understand?

From the perspective of journalists, who focus on how things look and are suspicious as a part of their occupation, it might be hard to comprehend that people, including politicians, are just living their lives and doing things that are in the end quite normal without thinking too much about strategy. From a cynical perspective, the fact that people are multidimensional may seem like too easy of an explanation. But there is no conflict between being professional and determined at work and silly and fun in private.

Everyone only has one life. I'm intending to live mine, and not to wait for some distant future to start. And I strongly believe that women have the right to be 100 percent who they are and shouldn't have to contort themselves to fit conservative, outdated standards designed to bring us down. I am not trying to provoke anyone, but I refuse to change myself just so I can look like a stereotypical politician.

Sometimes, people ask if I would have acted differently if I'd known beforehand that going to a party would cause such turbulence. I always find this question surprising, and I always respond the same way: What kind of life would that be?

## 11.

# WE ARE STILL FIGHTING

**We stand on the shoulders of those** who came before us. Before my term, Finland had had one female president, two female prime ministers, many female leaders of political parties, and many other courageous women who built our society and fought for the rights of women and children for decades. Each of these women made the path a little bit easier for those who came after her. The five female leaders of our government were able to rise to the top of the political hierarchy not only because of our own skills and commitment but also because of the sacrifices our predecessors made. Girls need examples of strong female leadership and we shouldn't underestimate the importance of role models. However, the roots for equal opportunities lie much deeper than this—in social structures that enable equal participation in education, welfare, and working life—and usually it has been the women together that have pushed these reforms within our societies.

The policies that have made Finland a front-runner in gender equality go back more than one hundred years. In 1906, Finland became the first country in the world to give women full political rights—not only the right to vote but also the right to run for office. Nineteen women were elected to our parliament the following year, and our first female minister, Miina Sillanpää, took office in 1926. Women's participation in decision-making was crucial in reforming our country into the welfare state it is today; having women in parliament and government meant there were always people in the room working on improving equality, education, and well-being. Ensuring the subjective right to affordable, high-quality daycare for children and social services for the elderly has freed women from unpaid care work and made it possible for them to participate in paid work and political activities. Something as simple as free school lunch, introduced in Finland in 1948, gave mothers the opportunity to work during the day instead of staying at home cooking—and providing nutritious meals for all schoolchildren has come with many secondary health and social effects that benefit the entire country. Paid maternity and parental leave has eased the burden on parents and enabled more women to pursue careers. Our maternity package—A Baby Box, a decades-old social innovation—provides families with baby clothes, care products, and other materials that a newborn needs. Numerous legislation changes over the decades have strengthened women's rights within families and communities and protected women from gender-based violence. These and many other changes in our society didn't come out of nowhere but were fought for—usually through long and hard battles in parliament and government by women who worked together side by side regardless of their political backgrounds.

Fighting for equality and parity is a constant struggle, and the stakes are incredibly high. Things that we, especially in Finland and other Nordic countries, take for granted, like sexual and reproductive health and rights, access to education and basic services, and living in a society that is based on democracy and the rule of law, are still dreams for many people worldwide. And the sad thing is that even in Finland, which is by all accounts one of the most equal countries in the world, women are still paid approximately 15 percent less than men, and over 50 percent of women have experienced physical and sexual violence or threats.

We have to remember that even though we have taken significant leaps toward equality over the past century, it can all disappear faster than we think. As I am writing this in 2025, we are witnessing severe backlash against women's rights globally. Women's and girls' rights to education, independence, services, and safety are degrading and even collapsing in many corners of the world. Sexual violence is being used as a tool of genocide and spreading fear among civilians in war and conflict zones. Women and children in Afghanistan, Yemen, Sudan, Palestine, Iran, Haiti, Ukraine, Syria, Myanmar, and many other places are paying an unforgivably high price for international ignorance, or maybe a lack of concern. And as we continue fighting for the things that women have fought for forever, we are also facing new challenges, like inequalities in the digital world. Whether it is the lack of access to information or digital tools, or the misogynist and hostile environment women face online, we have to address it as a political question—not only as a problem individuals face.

I have been asked many times how we can encourage women and younger generations to participate in politics. My answer is simple, but at the same time hard to deliver: we need a safe space in which to operate. If women face hostility when engaging in debate or political work, they are many times left to deal with this alone. Especially today, in the age of social media, threats come directly into women's homes through our screens. The number of people, real or fake, harassing women online is enormous. These aren't just isolated attacks but also targeted, widespread hate campaigns against people, mostly women and individuals from minority groups, just for speaking out. It is our job to make legislative and structural changes to put a stop to this, and the first step is to treat online harassment like any other type of violence.

It is no surprise that gender equality and human rights were high priorities in our government agenda. When I took office, twelve out of nineteen government ministers were women. We pushed through countless laws that have given women a stronger standing in working life and protection against violence, and dismantled structures that oppressed minority groups and those in weaker positions. We reformed parental leave legislation, made comprehensive reforms of sexual crime legislation and child protection legislation, transformed the Disability Service Act, reformed trans legislation as well as improved abortion rights, and made numerous other policy changes that aimed to strengthen people's physical and mental health, and their rights in workplaces, education, and welfare. Some might argue that rights for transgender people, sexual minorities, or indigenous people are trivial issues as they affect only a small group of citizens. But coming from an underprivileged background, and growing up around people who were discriminated against because of who they were and who they loved, I will always consider equality a core issue. When we focus on concrete reforms that give everyone equal rights and opportunities, we build a society that is better for all, not only those who are directly affected.

It is also no surprise that our women-led government faced misogyny and sexism throughout our term. We were given nicknames like the "lipstick government" or the "girl government," and we received endless streams of usually sexualized threats online. I have been threatened with rape and other types of sexual violence so many times that I can't even keep track. Our competence and ability to lead were questioned frequently, without justification. Our behavior was moralized about in a way that reminds me more of times when women weren't allowed to go out without male companions than the society we live in today. Our experiences reminded us that although we were a beacon of hope for many other countries, the double standards women face persist even in the most equal places in the world.

I have met many female leaders from all over the world, and one common theme in their stories is the loneliness they experienced as they have fought for their right to lead. For women, becoming a leader is always a struggle on many fronts, and we face obstacles and prejudice that men simply don't—and if you come from a minority ethnic background, or sexual or gender minority, or from a lower income class, you face even more obstacles. Inequality is a burden for individuals as well as for the collective good: when people with different backgrounds and experiences can't participate fully in society, we lose talent and knowledge that we need now more than ever.

The situations I've encountered for simply being myself while doing my job have sometimes been strange. One of the most bizarre—but clarifying—moments was in November 2022 in Auckland, New Zealand, at a joint press conference with Prime Minister Jacinda Ardern. A reporter asked us, the leaders of our respective countries, why we were meeting.

"A lot of people will be wondering: Are you meeting just because you are similar in age and got a lot of, hmmm, common stuff?"

I was baffled: This was really what a journalist wanted to ask me after I'd traveled twenty-eight hours to the other side of the world and spent an entire press conference discussing COVID-19 and the war in Ukraine? "We are meeting because we are prime ministers," I answered. The question was in a category of its own in terms of its absurdity, but not unique. I have been asked so many times about my age, gender, and being a parent, all things men in leadership positions never have to defend or even think about. Being a woman leader, and especially a young woman, is still atypical, and therefore newsworthy. This is the real problem: women represent half the population but only have a fraction of the world's power and resources.

I have met many talented male leaders, but *every* woman leader I have met has been talented. They've had to walk an extremely harsh path to get to the position they're in. But the challenges don't stop for women when they rise to the top; the double standards never go away, and we are pushed into the same tiny mold we've been in since childhood. There is pressure on women worldwide to be feminine, caring, soft, obedient, and adaptable. At the same time feminine characteristics are often considered weak, or vain. Leadership characteristics like ambition, strength, vision, talent, and credibility have historically been seen as masculine, and when women show these qualities they are considered "cold," "mean," "nasty," "unlikable." Women who show different sides of themselves, outside the expected roles, are not tolerated well. Nobody is the same at work and in their personal life, but for women, natural, normal code switching is seen as contradictory, and therefore somehow morally condemnable. But just like men, women are entitled to be fully themselves; strong, smart, and ambitious, and at the same time playful, sensitive, caring, and funny. When we wonder why women leave politics or why they are not eager to participate in the first place, perhaps we could first ask ourselves how we treat them.

○

I have learned many things while fighting for my own professional and personal space. I can relate to Mahatma Gandhi's famous saying: "First they ignore you, then they laugh at you, then they fight you, then you win." The harder the situation is, the more important it is not to give up. My motto, if I have one, is to cope through anything and fight for the things that really matter: a better world for our children and for the next generation. Hope is in our actions.

I have often made unexpected life choices. Given my background, I was never supposed to become a politician, and based on my career trajectory, it's a little surprising I changed the course of my life and left active politics before the age of forty. For me, 2023 was a year of change on all fronts. I believe that in order to truly open new doors, some old ones need to be closed.

Having led Finland through the pandemic, navigated our NATO process in the midst of the full-scale invasion of Ukraine, dealt with the daily struggles of a five-party coalition government, and still managed to implement 98 percent of our ambitious, reform-heavy government program, I was tired but at the same time ready for the parliamentary elections in April 2023. In the previous elections no one knew about the crises we would face during our four years in power, so this was the moment when the citizens could finally assess how we had fared.

Ours was a campaign Social Democrats hadn't experienced in a long time. Hundreds and even thousands of people gathered at our events all across Finland, where I toured with our ministers and candidates. This kind of turnout may be common in the United States, but in Finland, we don't love to participate in political rallies, so I was pleasantly surprised to see how passionately people supported us. Even though our party had managed to generate fairly good ratings in the polls throughout the term, and I was well appreciated among liberal and center-left supporters, I knew it would be difficult for us to win. In Finland, it's common for the opposition to make the strongest showing on the ballot. The reasons for this are understandable: because no party has the majority by itself, we always form coalitions, and in coalitions everyone has to compromise. This leads to ongoing negotiations, political disputes, and outcomes that are not always popular with each party's voters. But there is also political strength in coalition-based rule. Political shifts are rarely dramatic, because there is usually always at least one party in the coalition that served in the previous government, and parties are more used to working together than in systems in which two parties alternate in power.

The first real debates and campaign events started in January. After our party's campaign launch in February, I dedicated as much time to touring and meeting citizens as I possibly could while still performing all my other duties as prime minister. I was traveling frequently; the geopolitical situation hadn't cooled down, and Ukraine was still fighting for their independence and sovereignty. In March I visited Kyiv for the second time since the war started, and my statement about the possibility of assessing whether we could send our old fighter jets there was faced with heavy criticism, especially from the right. Another thing that got a controversial response was my strong stance that the SDP wouldn't negotiate or go to government with the Finns Party, a right-wing populist party. Their politicians had consistently expressed racist opinions, and we are so far apart in values and in political stances that I was just stating the obvious: we would never fit in the same coalition. But in Finland, people aren't used to this kind of categorical statement—all parties are expected to keep doors open to all possibilities. For me it was clear that some things are non-negotiable, like respect for human rights.

I knew that the only way for us to stay in the government would be if we finished first in the elections and led the negotiations. It was obvious that the right-wing National Coalition Party and the Finns Party had prepared a coalition well beforehand. I urged people to vote for us to make sure this didn't happen. The end result would be the most right-wing government Finland had ever had, and it would mean cuts to education, welfare services, and social benefits, as well as tax breaks for the rich, rising inequality, slowed or stalled climate action, and tightened immigration rules. Voting for the Social Democrats was the only way to prevent this from happening.

The race was extremely tight, but the end result was what I'd feared. The three leading parties finished within one percentage point of each other. The National Coalition Party won with 20.8 percent, the Finns Party was second at 20.1, and we finished third at 19.9. It was bittersweet: we had gained 2.2 percentage points more support than in the previous elections and won three more seats in parliament, but we lost the prime minister seat and the government.

I had mixed feelings about the results. I had done everything I could to win, and I knew how terrible the outcome was—what a right-wing government would mean for our country and our people. On this point, I was devastated. At the same time, I knew that this would allow me to reassess my direction in life. Leading the government during such a turbulent time had taken its toll on me on a personal level, and I was tired. My relationship with Markus, our marriage, was falling apart.

Markus and I had always had a very close connection, almost from the moment we met at age eighteen. But over the previous few years, it had gradually disappeared because my job was so intense and time-consuming. The daily conversations we used to have about life, the world, and all sorts of things had faded away. We lived under the same roof, but it felt like we were just passing by each other without ever stopping. My work drained my energy—I was often too tired to discuss what was going on, and sometimes I wasn't even allowed to say anything because it was classified or otherwise sensitive. Step by step, I closed myself off.

Because I was losing control over my personal life, I sought control where I could: my job, exercise, and morning routines. I usually woke up an hour before anyone else just to have a cup of coffee by myself, listen to music, and get ready for the day. This and reading a bedtime story to Emma were the things that I looked forward to, sometimes impatiently, every day. I realized I was also waiting for a period when I could spend more time with her. I missed her, and I felt guilty about not being able to give her the attention she deserved. I consoled myself that she was still young, and we had plenty of time ahead of us.

I remember the exact moment when I realized that the string between Markus and me had snapped. Nothing dramatic happened. No mistrust or disrespectful behavior. Just a clear realization that something irreversible had happened. I remember thinking about the Danish TV series *Borgen*, which is about a woman, Birgitte Nyborg, from a minority political party who becomes the prime minister of Denmark. A side plot in the series concerns Nyborg's marriage. At the beginning of the first season, she and her husband are a happy, powerful couple, but once she takes the job, their roles change, and they quickly drift apart. Their marriage ends by the end of the season. Years earlier, when I watched the show with Markus, neither of us could understand why they had sacrificed their relationship for the sake of her career. Now I could. It's not a conscious choice. It's just life.

From the outside, our separation might have seemed sudden, but these things rarely are. We didn't give up easily. For a long time we tried to fix what was broken. But it is impossible to restore a lost connection when you simply don't have time, and when resigning from your job is not an option. So we accepted that sometimes things end. I still consider him to be the best person I know, and I know he thinks the same about me. We have a beautiful daughter together, and we will be her loving parents forever, even if our relationship has changed.

○

My marriage wasn't the only thing that was ending. After the election result, I knew I needed to let go of some things to find myself again. I had always had such a passion for changing the world, but that had deteriorated as I got more and more tired. I felt like I had nothing left to give. No passion, no joy, no clear path to walk. A couple of days after the elections, I announced that I would not seek a second term in my leadership position at our party congress in September. I wanted to give other candidates enough time to campaign. Many people were surprised, but I'd always thought of myself as just one person among others, representing our values and aspirations. For me, it's the collective that matters, not my personal position. That's why stepping down wasn't a difficult choice, but a natural one. I was tired of being torn down by the press for years. I had coped with all the political difficulties and all the bullshit, and now it was time to make a choice of my own. I wanted to disappear from the limelight and constant scrutiny and just be me again. The media's interest in me had shifted beyond the professional, and my position was used as justification for their regular intrusions into my personal life. I always knew there was little I could do to stop the invasive reporting because it sold so well.

As I had assumed, after the elections, the National Coalition Party wanted to form a government with the Finns Party. They never tried to seriously negotiate with us. It took the parties forty-six days to agree on a program, almost twice as long as we had taken four years earlier, so I stayed in office until June 20, 2023. The two parties were accompanied by the Christian Democrats and the Swedish People's Party so that the government would have a majority in parliament.

The entire process of forming a new government took over two-and-a-half months, which for me felt like forever. Our government couldn't do anything anymore. So I concentrated on continuing to handle EU responsibilities and replying to some international requests to give speeches and attend interesting meetings and conferences. I especially remember giving a commencement speech to the New York University class of 2023 at Yankee Stadium in May. I had never spoken in front of such a large crowd—more than forty thousand graduates and their families and friends had come to celebrate the completion of their studies and the opening of new doors in their lives. I was happy to have the opportunity to give them some advice. I concluded on this note:

> *"There is no superior authority in this world giving us permission to be ourselves and to step forward to change the world. If I had waited for permission from others to take my stands, I would still be waiting for that permission. This is why my key advice to you today is not actually advice but a task: Stop being afraid."*

I wanted to live up to my own advice and not be afraid of the momentous change I was going through. When the former British prime minister Tony Blair contacted me and asked me to consider a role as a strategic counselor at his Institute for Global Change

(TBI), I replied that I would give it serious thought. It would mean having to resign from our parliament; I had just been re-elected with over thirty-five thousand votes from my constituency. This would cause a heated debate: in Finland, a parliamentarian can't just announce she is resigning; she needs permission from the parliament to do so. Still, I felt it was the right move for multiple reasons. As a former prime minister I would be in a difficult position working in ranks in parliament. I would be referred to and targeted in many debates, but I would not be able to reply and engage actively in the discussion. I couldn't be the one bashing the new government even though I would fiercely disagree with its policies. No senior position—as chair of a parliamentary committee or one of the speakers—felt suitable after serving as prime minister. I also didn't want to outshine our party's new leader—there was the risk that my presence would absorb too much oxygen. So I decided to take Blair up on his offer.

The institute's agenda is to help governments and leaders get things done by advising on strategy, policy, and delivery, with a special focus on technology across all three. I would be working on matters that were especially important to me. One of my key tasks would be advising Ukraine and Moldova in their aspirations to join the European Union. Some time after I took the job, the EU has officially opened accession negotiations with both countries, and we work with both governments to help them to reform their administrations to meet the accession criteria and build better, more resilient societies. I also advise leaders in other countries that the institute works with all across the world.

○

A week after our party congress, I called a press conference in the same hall of parliament where I'd held my first one, just after I was officially elected prime minister. As reporters gathered around me, I think everyone knew my announcement wouldn't be a small one. I told them I had been appointed to a new position in the Blair Institute and needed to resign from parliament. I was ready to open a new chapter in my life, and was leaving on my own terms. At the same time, I was sad to leave the job I had so passionately pursued and worked at, and I would miss all my colleagues, many of whom had become close friends over the years.

That evening I invited the same people to my apartment who had been there when our party voted for me to be the candidate for prime minister. Then, I had asked them "Do I really have to do this now?" without knowing anything that was to come. Now I just wanted to thank them for being there through everything we'd endured together. We ate, drank some wine, talked, cried, and laughed for hours as our children played around us. Even though I wasn't moving abroad or leaving the party, it felt like an ending of some sort. I would miss it all.

But when one door closes a new one opens. The day the parliament decided that it would grant me the resignation I had requested, a door that I couldn't wait to open was the one to my daughter's daycare. For years I had lived according to extremely tight schedules made by someone else, and many times I had been unable to do something as simple as pick her up. I'd decided I wasn't going to wake up one day only to realize that Emma had grown up and I had missed her childhood. I wanted my life to be more balanced between work and family.

I still travel heavily for work, but we live in Helsinki. I want Emma to have a Finnish education and a familiar environment to grow up in as there have been enough changes in her life already. She is with me every other week, and Markus and I are parenting as equally as possible. As I write this, she is practicing handstands in front of me and *Frozen* is playing in the background. I feel so fortunate to have more time with her.

What's next for me? I don't know, and that's the best part. I've never made a five- or ten-year plan, and I'm not going to start now. I know that I'll continue to try to change the world for the better in my own small ways, working on things that are close to my heart—supporting women, fighting for equality and human rights, and speaking about climate policy and the need to strengthen the international rules-based order. New opportunities will come and I can decide whether to embrace them or not. I consider myself lucky if my family and I are healthy and well, and if I've encouraged others to change things and make a difference.

# 12.

# HOPE IN THE SMALL MOMENTS

**The first step to making change** is facing reality. And the reality is that the world today does not look better than when I took office in 2019. The geopolitical landscape is in turmoil. International rules-based order is being challenged more and more, and in this age of "strong men" there are those who want to divide the world into spheres of influence once again. As countries cling to the comfort of national-ism, they are ignoring the fact that we need more joint action, not less, to combat major global challenges facing all of humanity such as climate change or the unimaginable speed of evolution in emerg-ing technologies such as AI, quantum or robotics. The success of the populist right-wing parties is not unusual, but increasingly, common. The re-election of President Donald Trump and the march of the far-right parties in many European countries are wake-up calls to anyone who cares about the values of justice, equality, sustainability, and welfare. Looking from Europe, it seems that the United States is abandoning its decades-long commitment to transatlantic relations and actively withdrawing from values-based cooperation. It simply does not make any sense why the once proud leader of the free world would want to weaken its own role and leave this power void to be filled by others, such as China.

Without a doubt, the world is becoming more unequal, and more dangerous for women and minority groups. The media environment gets more chaotic, and the hostility and misinformation that thrive on low-regulated social media platforms fuel the flames of authoritarianism and oppression. It's understandable to feel distraught, frustrated, scared, and confused—to wonder why everything we fought for, and gained, is being questioned, or even thrown away.

But the world isn't going to end, and it is only through action that we can feel hopeful again. Action doesn't have to be grand; we can all make a difference doing our own small part. Participation can give us the meaning and purpose in life that many are craving, especially in the current world situation.

According to research, helping others increases one's happiness. I argue that taking action, standing up for an important cause, speaking up for the values that matter and not focusing solely on ourselves, is not only important for society, but can actually have a profound impact on our own lives and well-being. We have a job to do.

In the meantime, change is a peculiar thing. Sometimes it's big and very noticeable, but sometimes it's evident in small moments. You have to pay attention, or you might not notice it's happening.

Once a year, every summer, political journalists are invited to Kesäranta for an off-the-record reception, with dinner and drinks, to acknowledge the important work they do as well as to give everyone an opportunity to contextualize complicated issues more freely. The atmosphere is usually playful; there are yard games and good food, and if the weather is decent people might use the sauna and swim in the sea. On the night of my first journalist reception, I put on my bathing suit and asked the female journalists to join me in the sauna, where we enjoyed high temperatures, occasionally dipping in cold water, and discussing politics, among all sorts of other things.

You could argue that saunas represent something about the Finnish approach to life: in saunas we come together as equals—title, background, or age doesn't matter. We are equally welcomed to enjoy the warmth and relax, just as our society is organized around the idea that everyone deserves to have more than just their basic needs met—we believe everyone deserves access to a good and healthy life.

In politics, however, the sauna has sometimes represented a kind of inequality. You're probably familiar with the image of businessmen or politicians in towels, sweating profusely as they negotiate deals in a dark, wooden room. Male-dominated saunas are a well-recognized political image. The myth and sometimes the truth is that real political decisions take place in saunas—the equivalent of a golf course or a locker room, just hotter and with more beer.

Male-exclusive spaces never play an official role in conversations about financial, economic, or political power. But we all know they exist. And we all know men probably took them for granted until women started speaking out against them, in whatever form that protest might take. That evening, we acted like it was a normal, casual thing to decamp to the sauna together as women, because it should be. But not everyone saw it that way.

At some point as we were cooling down in our towels outside, a male journalist came over to complain. He was upset that his female colleagues got to spend so much more time with me, the prime minister, in a place where the men couldn't follow. They had been left out of the discussions.

"I know exactly how you feel," one of the female journalists replied.

The issue wasn't that the man wanted everyone to go to the sauna at the same time. It's customary that men and women take turns going to the sauna when people attending events like this aren't close friends or family members. Rather, the men had experienced something that women are so accustomed to: the feeling of being excluded from power and knowledge.

"I could get used to this," that female journalist said to me, feeling powerful and in control. I gave her a smile and realized that although our female-led government was still the exception rather than the norm, it had the power to change the world.

# ACKNOWLEDGMENTS

So many people have helped, guided, supported, challenged, and stood by me on this journey. They all deserve to be acknowledged and thanked individually, but I am painfully aware that that might be impossible to do in a limited number of pages.

What an absolute privilege it has been to work with such talented and good-hearted people. We might not have always seen eye to eye, but you have definitely pushed me forward, and I am grateful. I have learned something from each one of you.

This book has been made possible thanks to the hard work of many. First of all I want to thank my editor Kara Watson at Scribner for her guidance, insights, and help. Writing this book has been an exciting, fun, overwhelming and intense process, and I could not have asked for a more brilliant editor.

I am forever grateful to Margaret Riley King and Laura Bonner at WME who helped me take a leap into the unknown. Thank you for your kind encouragement and support during our collaboration. Many thanks also to Matilda Forbes Watson and the rest of the team.

Thank you Lauren Oyler for helping me to structure and refine my story. You helped me find the stories that needed to be told. And of course I really appreciate your help with my English grammar!

I want to especially thank my two former advisors, Tuulia Pitkänen and Iida Vallin. Tuulia, with your support we were able to make the first moves and bring this idea to life. I have had the privilege of working with you for many years, and I am forever thankful for your dedication. Iida, you have kept everything together and decisively moving forward. Thank you for always staying cool, calm, and collected even in the most pressured situations.

Without this bunch of dear friends and former advisors, the writing process would have been much more difficult. Henrik Haapajärvi, Jari Luoto, Mikko Koskinen, Matti Niemi, Joonas Rahkola, Pirita Ruokonen, and Lauri Voionmaa—I am so immensely grateful for your kind help. You have read and commented on chapters (sometimes in a really hectic schedule!) and helped me to make this book better. I am honored to have you on my team.

Thank you so much Scribner and the outstanding team: Sophie Guimaraes, Jaya Miceli, Marysue Rucci, Paul Samuelson, Stu Smith, and Brianna Yamashita.

Thank you Johanna Vehkoo for your diligent work with fact checking and Johanna Laitinen for your kind support.

Meeri Koutaniemi is one of the most talented photographers and I want to thank you for your amazing work with the cover photo. It was so lovely to work with the whole photoshoot team: Satu Arvo, Liisa Kokko, Arttu Kokkonen, Jussi Pyykkönen, Saila Semeri, and Joni Willberg. Thank you very much, Andiata, for lending me the beautiful power suit.

Beyond this book, I had the opportunity and honor to work with many hardworking, talented, and exceptional people during my term as a prime minister and party leader. They deserve of course to be acknowledged.

First, I want to sincerely thank the leaders of the governmental parties Li Andersson, Anna-Maja Henriksson, Katri Kulmuni, Maria Ohisalo, and Annika Saarikko. You are great politicians and brilliant people. It has been a privilege to work with you during these turbulent years.

My heartfelt thanks to the other ministers of my government: Thomas Blomqvist, Tuula Haatainen, Pekka Haavisto, Timo Harakka, Petri Honkonen, Antti Kaikkonen, Emma Kari, Krista Kiuru, Hanna Kosonen, Antti Kurvinen, Jari Leppä, Aki Lindén, Mika Lintilä, Krista Mikkonen, Sirpa Paatero, Aino-Kaisa Pekonen, Jussi Saramo, Hanna Sarkkinen, Mikko Savola, Ville Skinnari, Tytti Tuppurainen, and Matti Vanhanen. I am deeply proud of the work we did together during our governmental term. I know I speak for all of us when I say that it was such an honor to serve our country.

My sincere appreciation and thanks to the former prime minister and party leader Antti Rinne for your support and dedicated work for our goals and aspirations.

My warmest thanks to the president Sauli Niinistö for your work and our partnership, especially during the historic NATO process. I am proud of the cooperation of the whole state leadership and parliament in a very dire situation that required unity and determination.

I want to thank my former advisors for the expertise and endless support you gave me during my term as prime minister. You are pure gold. Not already mentioned: Kirsi Airio, Lauri Finér, Elisa Gebhard,

Ilkka Hamunen, Ilkka Kaukoranta, Iiris Niinikoski, Saara Pokki, Dimitri Qvintus, and Niilo Toivonen.

Miia Maffeo and Riitta Mäkelä, my trusted and excellent secretaries, thank you so much for everything you do. Heartfelt thanks also to Sara Holappa, Noora Kettunen, and Sanna Laakso.

My sincere thanks to all the dedicated civil servants in the Prime Minister's Office, in other ministries, and in the Parliament. Your efforts were remarkable, especially during the COVID-19 crisis and our NATO process. Although it is impossible to name everyone, here are a few individuals I want to especially thank for your outstanding efforts during the COVID crisis: Tuula Kulovesi, Timo Lankinen, Taneli Puumalainen, Tuomas Pöysti, Mika Salminen, Kirsi Varhila, and Liisa-Maria Voipio-Pulkki. I want to also thank my security team, drivers, House Manager of Kesäranta and the other great staff working in Kesäranta, Säätytalo, the Prime Minister's Office, and the Parliament.

My profound gratitude for Antton Rönnholm, who made sure that everything kept moving forward within our party. Thank you very much, Niina Malm, Matias Mäkynen, and Ville Skinnari for your hard work and support. I want to thank people working in the Party Office and regions for your dedication and efforts for reaching our goals and aspirations. I want to also express my gratitude to my colleagues at the Tampere city council for their support and encouragement.

Warm thanks to Antti Lindtman and to our whole parliamentary group for valuable and good cooperation. I will always cherish your support during my term as prime minister, it meant the world to me. My sincere thanks goes also to Kari Anttila and our excellent staff working at the Parliamentary Group.

SDP party members and activists: it has been an honor to work with you for a better and more equal society. We shall keep fighting for a brighter future together.

I want to also share my deepest thanks to Magdalena Andersson. I truly valued our excellent cooperation during our NATO process and the fact that we could always have honest and trusted discussions with each other. Warm thanks also to Jens Stoltenberg for great cooperation.

I want to thank my dear prime minister colleagues from the Nordic and Baltic countries for our wonderful partnership. Sincere thanks also to Ursula von der Leyen, Charles Michel, and my colleagues with whom I had the pleasure to work within the European Union.

And last, I don't know where I would be without the unwavering support and love from my family and close friends.

My dear friends and former colleagues Krista Kiuru, Suna Kymäläinen, and Ilmari Nurminen. How could I ever describe what your support has meant to me during these years? For better and for worse, you have stood by me and helped me carry on. For that I am forever thankful.

My friends Maria Mäkynen, Nelli Nurminen, and Nasima Razmyar. Life is busy and we don't always find the time to catch up as often as we would like, but when we do, it feels like no time has passed. Thank you for your friendship.

My deepest appreciation and love goes to Markus Räikkönen, who has supported, loved, and encouraged me. I am so grateful that I had the privilege of sharing my life with you for so many years, and that we have a beautiful daughter together.

Emma, you are my greatest joy. I am so proud of you. You bring such love to my life that I never knew existed before I had you. I am eagerly awaiting all the adventures we will have together. When I look at you I see hope in action.

Finally, it is hard to put into words how grateful I am to my mother. You have always been there for me and helped me to trust myself. You have encouraged me to take action and rooted me with the values that have guided everything I do. Thank you.